from S

GW01090524

3

Medit

Women Who

Spend Too Much

Celestial Keys to Financial Serenity

Jane Bowles
Lightworks Press

Meditations for Women Who Spend Too Much

ISBN 0 – 9539455 – 0 – 2

First published by Lightworks Press 2003
Copyright © Jane Bowles 2003

Jane Bowles asserts the moral right to be identified as the author
of this work

Book design and typesetting by LA Business Images, Sidmouth
Cover design by LA Business Images, Sidmouth
Cover image Copyright © 2003 Lightworks Press Ltd
and its licensors. All rights reserved.

Lightworks Press Ltd, 109 Winslade Road, Sidmouth, Devon, EX10 9EZ
Tel no: (44) 01395-516409; fax: (44) 01395-579973
E-mail: jane @janebowles.fsworld.co.uk

Distributed to the book trade in the UK through Airlift Book Company,
8 The Arena, Mollison Avenue, Enfield, Middx, EN3 7NL.

Distributed to the book trade in the USA through New Leaf Distributing Co,
401 Thornton Road, Lithia Springs, GA 30122-1557.
www.newleaf-dist.com

Dedication

This book is dedicated to my children,

Lucie and Alexander

and to the memory of my father

Disclaimer

The author of this book does not dispense financial advice, nor prescribe the use of any financial technique as a remedy for financial problems. The intent of the author is only to offer information of a general nature to help readers in their quest for financial well-being. In the event that you use any of the information in this book for yourself, the publisher and author assume no responsibility for your actions.

Acknowledgments

In the process of bringing this book into being, so many people have helped me in so many ways that it would be an impossible task to list them all. However, my heartfelt thanks must go to the following: to Eileen Caddy, co-founder of the Findhorn Foundation for her inspiration and kindness; and to Lesley Anderson of LA Business Images, for her patience, creative flair and technical brilliance!

Thanks also to Rob Harford, for encouraging me to get the first draft written; to Tracey and Oscar Hammond, Vicki Campbell and Nikki Marshall for their help and support during the initial stages of writing; to Noelle Worsley, Sue Telfer, Joyce Lucas, Jet Izabella Thurman, Trish Sulaimani, Hugh Benson and Helena Francis for their continuing support and encouragement.

Thanks also to my children, Lucie and Alexander, for their lovely drawings, and for patiently enduring my long disappearances into "Mummy's work-room"- and to my mother, for her support on every imaginable level. And finally, to my "soul-sister" Janet Ekaette, for her unfailing support, stalwart friendship and boundless spiritual wisdom. Without her support, this book would truly never have been written!

Contents

Introduction

"We're zealots at pursuing financial security when what we really hunger for is financial serenity. Financial serenity is never having to worry about money again because you've discovered the true Source... Financial serenity starts when we accept as our truth that money is a state of mind, and that abundance is a state of belief... When we choose abundance ... we attain true Wealth."

Sarah Ban Breathnach

This book evolved out of a talk I gave at the groundbreaking Findhorn Foundation Conference, "Business For Life", entitled "Astrology, Money and You: The Twelve Spiritual Lessons of Money". Thank you, Eileen Caddy, for suggesting that I come and speak at Findhorn – and thanks to Johnny O'Brien, the Conference Facilitator, for helping plant the seeds that grew into this book.

My invitation to speak at Findhorn not only inspired the writing of this, my third book on the fascinating links between astrology and money – it also marked the beginning of my own journey towards financial serenity. For although at the time, I was making a reasonable living as a consultant astrologer and free-lance journalist, for me personally, money remained a huge and troublesome issue. Organising my finances was a task that I found overwhelming, and it seemed virtually impossible to save money or live within my means. However much I earned, it always seemed like I needed "more"... I'd take on writing assignments I didn't really feel like doing - "just for the money"- and then spend the extra money buying things I didn't really need - "just to cheer myself up"...

Each month brought its own agenda of balancing current expenses with the need to honour past commitments, and I spent a great deal of time juggling my various bank accounts. I made my living writing and speaking about finance, but in my own life, money operated like an elemental force; like a wild beast that could not be tamed. The irony of my situation was not lost on me, but I felt powerless to change it. In short, money felt like a riddle that I simply could not solve...

Help was at hand, however, and it came to me at Findhorn. The day after giving my presentation, I was browsing in the Foundation bookshop, when I came across a stack of books on simple living and downshifting. The ideas of authors such as Vicki Robin and Joe Dominguez, Elaine St. James and Amy Dacyczyn were totally new to me, but they all embodied a common message of "less is more". On returning home, I began to experiment with handling my finances in a different, more conscious way – initially by the simple technique of writing down everything I spent, and analysing exactly where my hard-earned money was going... Within weeks I was able to plug the "black holes" in my spending, and for the first time in years, I began to feel relaxed about money. The ideas I discovered at Findhorn set in motion a process of financial healing, and gradually, the abundance I was experiencing on an inner level began to be reflected in my outer life...

Since that time, I've continued to refine my own ideas about "living well on less", and I'm delighted to be able to share these with you in this book. As a practising astrologer, my experience has shown me that our star sign has a significant influence on how we relate to money, and also on the kinds of issues and lessons that each of us are likely to encounter. Readers can rest assured that I have personally tried and tested all the ideas and exercises featured in this book!

How should you best use this book? You would naturally want to read the meditations for your own sign first, but since we each have a little bit of all the twelve signs lurking within us, I would also recommend that you read all the other signs too, and do any of the exercises that it feels appropriate to do. It's also a good idea to buy a small notebook to do the exercises in, and for charting your own progress.

Finally, if there's one fundamental lesson my own journey has taught me, it's that the more we devote ourselves to becoming who we truly are, the more we will find our lives becoming filled with prosperity and abundance. This is the ultimate spiritual lesson of money, and it applies to us all, no matter what sign we were born under. Enjoy!

Jane Bowles
Sidmouth, Devon
September 2002

♈

Aries

"I want what I want when I want it."

Henry Blossom

Intuition

"Money never starts an idea. It is the idea that starts the money."

W J Cameron

As the first fire sign of the zodiac, we Ariens are blessed with excellent powers of intuition, as well as the courage to act on our inner promptings. Creativity guru Julia Cameron calls these promptings, "marching orders" – and they usually appear in our lives to show us our next step.

What life requires of us is that we pay attention to that magical power of intuition we possess, and follow its wisdom. Our intuition can help us by giving us the inspiration for a new business or creative project, or through finding a new business partner. Or simply through a contact, a dream, or maybe just an undeniable sense of conviction about the next move we need to make.

If we follow our intuition, we help to expand the flow of prosperity and abundance in our lives. If we ignore our intuition, the reverse tends to happen, and the flow of our lives becomes stymied and "stuck". All great success stories started out as an idea. What's yours?

"I am now willing to listen to my intuition."

Honouring Creativity

*"Why should we all use our creative power? ...
Because there is nothing that makes people so
generous, joyful, lively, bold and compassionate,
so indifferent to fighting and the accumulation
of objects and money."*

Brenda Ueland

As Ariens, we are the pioneer sign of the zodiac, and in accordance with our true inner nature, we need to be constantly sowing the seeds of new ideas, concepts and ventures. If we are simply living out someone else's dreams and visions, we will never be happy, and we need to acknowledge that.

We need to say our own creative thing, and say it in our own unique way – or at least, have a sense that we are able to work towards this sense of inner freedom. Otherwise, it's easy for us to fall into the trap of spending money simply to compensate ourselves for the lack of satisfaction we feel in our lives.

Today, take your notebook and make a list of those areas where you feel you have a unique, creative contribution to make – where you can break new ground, and be your true pioneering Arien self. There, that feels better, doesn't it?

"I now allow myself to express my creative spirit."

Strategy

*"In preparing for battle, I have found that plans
are useless, but planning is indispensable!"*
            Dwight D Eisenhower

We Ariens are among the great movers and shakers of the
zodiac, and we like to make things happen. But our need
to see quick – if not instant – results, can sometimes cause
a great deal of time and money to get wasted in false starts.

Money spent on training courses or new business start-ups
that we don't persevere with can, in the long run, add up
to a lot of squandered resources. Looking back on a whole
series of so-called "failures" can also undermine our confidence and self-esteem, and can make us feel like we have
achieved very little in our lives.

A good antidote lies in developing a long-term strategy
and game plan. We may not feel that planning is our strong
point – but it is a skill that's focal to the path of financial
serenity, and so it's one we need to master. Remember, "P"
for planning comes before "R" for results in the dictionary!

Today, take your notebook and write out a list of your
business and financial goals, and the steps you need to
take in order to achieve them. Start working on your long-
term work and financial plan today.

**"I am now willing to take a long-term view
of my finances."**

Enthusiasm

"People are always good company when they are doing what they really enjoy."

Samuel Butler

If we want to boost our earning power, then enthusiasm for what we are doing is totally indispensable to the process. The roots of the word "en" and "theos" literally mean "filled with divinity" – and when we do what we love, the Spirit shines through us, and illuminates everything we do. Conversely, when we aren't doing what we love, we are far more likely to fritter our time, energy and money away at the nearest shopping mall...

If you don't feel you are making enough room in your life for the things you love to do, take some time today to rediscover where your true enthusiasm lies. What did you love to do as a child and a teenager? What would you gladly do without being paid for it, just for the sheer joy of doing it? What are your hobbies? And so on...

Today, promise yourself that you will make time at least twice a week to renew your acquaintance with an old pastime you once had boundless enthusiasm for. In time, the joy you experience will spill over into every other area of your life...

"I now make time for activities that fill me with enthusiasm."

Patience

"Patience is the companion of wisdom."

St Augustine

Ah, that's so true, n-est-ce pas? As Ariens, we feel our blood runs hotter and faster than that of less feisty mortals. Quite frankly, when we decide we want something, having it yesterday wouldn't have been soon enough! But the truth is, life doesn't always unfold at top speed … and we need to allow sufficient time for creative ideas and projects to develop at their own pace.

It can be helpful if we think of our lives as a garden. When we act on an idea, it's a bit like planting a seed. When we plant seeds, we don't expect them to flower overnight. And when the shoots start to appear, we don't rip them up by the roots to see if they're growing, do we? Applying this kind of "green logic" to our business and financial endeavours can help us overcome our tendency to be impatient. But just don't expect to become patient overnight!

"I am now willing to allow time for my projects to unfold."

Spending Plans

"Take the time to come up with other solutions to your next perceived buying need, or at the very least, wait for a few days to let the immediate gratification impulse lose its hold on you..."

Elaine St James

When it comes to shopping, "I want it, and I want it now" is the Aries house motto, and impulse spending is our biggest retail downfall. But living so totally in the moment is NOT the surest route to fiscal bliss, because all those last-minute purchases have a way of catching up with us. In black and white, on next month's credit card statement...

What can help us overcome this tendency to impulsiveness? It helps if we go to cash. Allow yourself a fixed amount for spending each week, and take it out of the bank in cash when you want to go shopping. Leave your credit cards and cheque book at home. Ouch! I know, I know ... but you don't have to do it forever.

If you see something you want that you can't afford right now, write it on a piece of paper or in your notebook, for purchase in the future. This simple technique of delaying gratification helps us create a spending plan, and gets us used to the idea of planning our purchases. And in a few days time, we may even find that we no longer want the item, or that we've come up with some kind of alternative!

"I now create a spending plan."

Debt Management

"Cutting down on how much you pay for the privilege of using borrowed money is a cardinal rule of saving money. After all, you've already done your time at the office for the privilege of having money. Why pay again, and drag the ball and chain of debt around too, as you hobble down the road of life?"

Joe Dominguez and Vicki Robin

With credit cards available so freely, and rates of borrowing on occasion running as high as 25 – 30%, lessening our dependence on borrowed money is essential to our quest for financial serenity. Leaving your credit cards at home when out shopping is one way, but if you really can't resist temptation, you may find the only thing to do is to go "cold turkey" and chop 'em up.

I did this "plastic surgery" back in the early 1990s, and it proved to be quite a personal turning point for me and my finances. If you feel your credit card debts have become unmanageable, you might want to write to the companies involved and see if you can negotiate a lower rate of borrowing while you pay back the debt. But watching your debt melt away, as your finances slowly emerge into the black and leave the scarlet zone behind, is a totally satisfying experience, I promise you!

"I now allow myself to live within my means."

Focus

"The will is meant to guide you … so that what-
ever is appropriate for any situation is what you
feel like doing."

Ceanne Derohan

Whatever we are aiming to do, whether it's a business ven-
ture that we want to bring to fruition, or simply the task of
cleaning up our act around money, we need to learn to concentrate. With feisty, dynamic Mars as our planetary ruler,
however, that's sometimes easier said than done.

What will help us to improve our focus? Sport is often a
good training ground for the Arien will, and can help us
develop concentration, so that we don't get distracted from
our chosen path. It can even help us stick to our spending
plan!

Do you have a favourite sport? Ariens often love to run,
and many people report entering a kind of trancelike state
as they cover familiar ground in their daily circuit. Tennis
is another sport that can help improve your powers of concentration. Today, resume your practice of an old,
favourite sport, or give yourself the pleasure of taking up
a new one. So choose a sport. Just do it!

"I am now able to concentrate on the
task in hand."

Asking

"Ask, and it shall be given unto you: seek, and ye shall find; knock, and it shall be opened unto you."

Matthew 7:7

Asking for what we want in life is such a simple idea really, but so few of us seem to remember to do it. We don't ask the bank for a loan to start our own business, we don't ask the boss for a raise, we don't ask our children to be quiet so we can read a book in peace, we don't ask our partners to help out with the household chores, and so on...

It is a principle of universal law, however, that if we don't ask for what we want, we most certainly AREN'T going to get it. We are then rather like a boat that's set out to sea without a rudder – and sometimes even without a pair of oars! As Ariens, we know that we want things to happen, but we need to be clear and precise in our own minds about WHAT those things are. I like Stuart Wilde's take on this. He says that life is like a restaurant, and if you don't place your order, the food just isn't coming...

"I am now willing to ask for what I want in my life."

Goal Setting

"It is my experience that putting wishes on the page begins to put them in motion."

Julia Cameron

Once we have gotten clear about what we want, the next step is to commit those wants to paper. I don't know why this should be so, but there is just something about the process of writing our dearest dreams and wishes down on paper that seems to get them moving along the path to realization.

Today, take your notebook and write out a "wish list". The items on your list can apply to any area of your life that you choose – whether it's getting a promotion, finding the perfect couch for your living room, or paying off your debts. Be sure to date your list, and go back and look at it in six months time. You'll be amazed at just how many of your "wishes" have been granted. Alice Anne Parker, the first astrologer I ever knew, taught me this valuable exercise. She lives in Hawaii now, and I'm sure that move was on her list!

"I commit my dreams to paper, and in so doing, I commit myself to my dreams."

Self Employment

"What's money? A man is a success if he gets up in the morning, goes to bed at night, and does what he wants to do in between."

Bob Dylan

We Ariens are rarely happy when being told what to do by other people. With dynamic Mars as our planetary ruler, being able to run our own show really matters to us a lot. So we need to work towards being in a situation where we can dictate our own routine, take the risks we want to take, and just call the proverbial shots.

As a general rule, we do have the energy to do this, but when we feel that our lives are being overly controlled by others, we fall prey to lassitude and depression.

Even if starting your own business or going freelance seems like an impossible goal right now, if this is your dream, you need to start finding out how you could go about it, and start saving money towards it. Even just a small amount of money each month helps. The act of moving towards a goal in a state of faith tends to spark the support of the universe. Try it!

"I now accept responsibility for my own destiny."

Inner Peace

"Instead of fighting against your circum-stances, learn to flow with them and so find that inner peace and understanding deep within".

Eileen Caddy

"Aries loveth nothing above a victory" observed the 17th Century astrologer William Lilly, and this maxim still holds all too true today. We Ariens can get pretty addicted to the cut and thrust of competition for its own sake, or get caught up in one-upping our neighbour and workmate just for the hell of it.

If competition and conflict have become a way of life for you, be aware that you're dissipating valuable energy that could perhaps be more creatively employed elsewhere. Spending quiet time each day helps us to connect with our intuition, as well as helping us feel more peaceful. Thus we can help ourselves to cultivate that elusive, but desirable quality of inner peace and serenity…

"I now make it a priority to spend quiet time each day."

♈ ♉ ♊ ♋ ♌ ♍ ♎ ♏ ♐ ♑ ♒ ♓

♉

Taurus

"It is better to have a permanent income than to be fascinating."

Oscar Wilde

Plenitude

*"Wealth consists not in having great posses-
sions, but in having few wants."*

Epicurus BC 341 – 270

We Taureans are ruled by Venus, the goddess of beauty,
ease and luxury, and our house motto is very often "more
is better". More money in the checking account, more food
in the refrigerator, more perfumed goodies in the bath-
room, etc, etc. But our acquisitive nature can sometimes
become a kind of trap, as we get caught in the relentless
cycle of earning more and more to sustain and maintain
the "more" that we already have...

Today, take a notebook and write out a list of what would
constitute "enough" for you. You could discover that
maybe you don't really want more consumer goods after
all – but simpler, intangible things. Like for instance, more
time to spend with your loved ones, longer vacations, time
for hobbies, etc. Take time in writing out your list, and you
will find out what "enough" really means to you...

**"I am now willing to experience a sense
of plenitude in my life."**

Inner Truth

"Often people attempt to live their lives back-wards: they try to have more things, or more money, in order to do more of what they want so that they will be happier. The way it works is actually the reverse. You must first be who you really are, then do what you need to do, in order to have what you want."

Margaret Young

All too often, we Taureans think we have to build a rock-solid foundation of unassailable financial security before we can permit ourselves the luxury of exploring our God-given talents and creative potential. We tell ourselves, "I'll make my stash, and then I'll take a year off and travel round the world, or write that novel. I'll do the things I want when I've got enough money in the bank…" But the truth is, our gifts and abilities – those things we love to do above all else – are very often a surer route to wealth than the path of "being practical".

Taking the road less travelled, and turning our thinking around in this manner is a hard shift for us to make – but when we support ourselves by doing what we love, doors swing open as if by magic, and the universe will support us in far more ways than we can ever imagine.

*"I now allow myself to be who I really **am**."*

Simplicity

"Simplifying is not necessarily about getting rid of everything we've worked so hard for. It's about making wise choices among the things we now have to choose from."

Elaine St James

One consequence of falling into the Taurean trap of thinking we must have it all before we can relax into becoming who we truly are, is that our lives (and houses) can get amazingly cluttered! The fact is big houses and big cars need more time and money in order to maintain them – and if we'd far rather be painting pictures or writing poetry, do we really need all that stuff anyway?

Elaine St James, author of "Simplicity", made the leap into a refreshingly uncluttered lifestyle when she and her husband Gibbs gave away a great many of their possessions to charity and moved to a much smaller apartment. The result? More time and energy to do the things they really wanted to do. We all have choices – so take some time today to explore the implications of your own spending decisions up until now. Would a simpler lifestyle serve the "real you" better?

"I surround myself only with those objects and possessions that serve my true purpose in life."

Spendfasting

"Don't go shopping. If you don't go shopping, you won't spend money. Of course, if you really need something from the store, go and buy it. But don't just go shopping."

Joe Dominguez and Vicki Robin

In her book, "Women Who Shop Too Much", Carolyn Wesson states that "59 million persons in the United States are addicted to shopping or to spending. In addition, about 53 per cent of grocery buys and 47 per cent of hardware store purchases are said to be "spur of the moment".

Are YOU the kind of person who goes shopping as a kind of leisure pursuit or hobby, and who carries on browsing and buying out of habit, even though you already have far more than you need? If you're in doubt put yourself on a spendfast. Don't buy anything (apart from groceries and essential items for children, if you have them) for thirty days – and don't go grocery shopping without a list. Cutting down on the number of trips to the store helps too, as it means you'll have less exposure to temptation. This simple exercise will show you very clearly where you may be squandering your money…

"I am willing to forego all nonessential purchases for 30 days."

Taurus

True Wealth

"There are those who are wealthy, and those who are rich."

Coco Chanel

Now that we have a bit more time on our hands, thanks to the spendfast, let's do some serious thinking! As an earth sign, we Taureans tend to count our wealth only in terms of what we can see – the house, the cars, the art collection, etc. – but the truth is, we are all blessed with a truly massive amount of intangible wealth too. This constitutes our "Invisible Bank Account".

Here's an example. What good would all the money in the world be to us if we didn't possess our health, so that we could enjoy the wealth we've been blessed with? What about the unseen web of love and support of our partners, parents, friends and family that surrounds and sustains us? And what of our "invisible inventory" – our gifts for commerce and language, our musical ability, our love of travel, the friends and contacts we've made along the way... Take time today to calculate your true wealth. You could be surprised to discover how rich you really are...

"I am now conscious of the true wealth that fills my life."

Gratitude

"Give thanks for everything you have, for everything you receive, and for everything you are going to receive. In fact, never cease to give thanks, for it is a positive attitude towards life, and the very act of giving thanks which draw the very best to you."

Eileen Caddy

It seems to be a kind of universal cosmic principle that the more you take time to appreciate what you do have, the more you seem to be given! We Taureans don't always remember to take the time to do this, as we find it so hard to break our allegiance to the Law of More … if you've been sticking to the spendfast, however, you should have some time to spare this week.

Take your notebook, and write out a list of twenty things you are grateful for in your life right now – regardless of the state of your bank balance, or any feelings of frustration you may have if your career isn't progressing as quickly as you'd like. Just the mere act of writing out the list should give you a warm inner glow and a delicious sense that "all's right with the world". As an ongoing practice, incorporate an attitude of gratitude into your life by writing out three things you are grateful for each night before you go to sleep. You can write out more if you wish to, but do write out at least three…

"I now give thanks for all the good things in my life."

31

Delight

"Whoever said money can't buy happiness didn't know where to shop."

Gertrude Stein

Today, I'd like you to focus on the art of conscious shopping. But don't think I'm encouraging you to go out and become a shophound all over again. Rather, I'm extending you an invitation to discover what truly delights you in your life...

In their groundbreaking book, "Your Money Or Your Life", Joe Dominguez and Vicki Robin tell us that frugality is essentially about getting good value for every minute of your life energy – that precious commodity that you are really trading when you spend your money. By inference, this means only buying those things that truly give you pleasure and thus getting true value for the money that you spend.

What is it that gives you delight? A huge bunch of flowers from the farmer's market, a bottle of lavender oil for your bath, the ingredients for a delicious candlelit supper for two? Today, take some time to really consider the things that you most love in life. If these are things that you can buy, be sure to treat yourself to at least one of them next time you go shopping...

"I now purchase only those goods and services that truly delight me."

Sharing

"Money is like muck: pile it up and it stinks, spread it around and it makes things grow."

Anonymous

A truly magical law of the universe is the principle that the more we give away, the more we seem to be given… But since we Taureans tend to be far fonder of piling up money and possessions almost indefinitely, this is not an idea that tends to really "grab" us. "Give it away? All that stuff I've worked so hard for? Well, maybe at Christmas and on birthdays, but the rest of the time? I don't think so"…

Taking a higher, bird's-eye perspective of the whole process of life, however, we can begin to understand that everything we have is on loan from the universe anyway – even our bodies, which will one day be returned to Mother Earth. All our possessions, houses and land too, will one day be owned by somebody else. It's quite a thought, isn't it?

So, in the meantime, practise "letting go" by sharing what you already have. Give to charity whenever you can. Invite friends over to dinner, and if a friend admires your best vase, muster the grace to make them a gift of it. Remember the words of Kahlil Gibran: "Money is like love: it kills slowly and painfully the one who withholds it, and enlivens the other who turns it on his fellow men."

"I am now willing to share a part of all I own."

Insight

"Get to know two things about a woman. How she earns her money and how she spends it. You will then have the clue to her character. You will have a searchlight that shows up the innermost recesses of her soul. You know all you need to know about her standards, her motives, her driving desires, her real religion."

Robert McCracken

I once attended a lecture on Prosperity by the spiritual teacher Paul Solomon where he stated that if you wanted to know what a person really valued in life, you had only to look at their chequebook stubs. It's true, isn't it? What we spend our money on speaks volumes about our true priorities. If we are spending all our money on mortgage payments for our new house, then we value that house more than anything else, don't we? How we spend our money shows us what we really value in life more clearly than almost any other aspect of our behaviour. The chequebook does not lie!

Today, take time to analyse your expenditure and evaluate your "real religion" as reflected in your spending patterns. Is it houses? Food? Clothes? Drugs? Your Mercedes? Or do you spend it on your children, your spiritual development, or your loved ones? Where does it all go? Take some time to explore this...

"I am now willing to examine my spending patterns."

Seasonal Harmony

"If you don't insist on having grapefruit in the summer and peaches in the winter, you can lower your grocery bill significantly. Remember the law of supply and demand. What is plentiful will be cheaper. What is scarce will be more expensive. Don't break that law, and you won't end up broke."

Joe Dominguez and Vicki Robin

A witty astrologer once remarked that what any Taurus woman really wants out of life is "good food, good sex and a nice place to live" – and I think most Taureans would agree with that remark. Since good food can often account for such a major portion of the Taurean budget, however, mastering the art of eating in harmony with the seasons is essential to keeping your food bills as low as possible, without sacrificing your love of good food.

The great bonus of taking the seasonal approach is also that you can expand your repertoire of recipes instead of sticking to the tried and tested stuff. Find out what's in season, get some new cookery books and experiment a little. As master chef Ruth Rogers, co-author of the River Café Cook Book comments, "it's pointless eating strawberries flown in from South Africa in January because they won't taste of anything."

"I now practise good nutrition in harmony with the seasons."

Natural Wonder

"My soul can find no staircase to heaven unless it be through earth's loveliness."

Michelangelo

Taurus is the sign of fixed earth, and when a Taurean feels they've been spending too much money because their life is out of whack, one of the very best remedies of all is to pack up a rucksack and a good strong pair of walking boots and head for the hills – or wherever your favourite place of natural beauty happens to be.

For most Taureans find that being in nature is a true healing balm, and one that usually needs to be applied every weekend, at the very least. Taureans with a strong water emphasis in their horoscope might prefer to take a walk by the seashore: or, if you've more air planets in your chart, you might prefer your countryside spiced up with some hills or even the odd mountain range! Either way, spending time in nature will usually restore you to a state of equilibrium.

"I now restore my spirits through enjoying the beauty of nature."

Cosmic Harmony

"Study the cycles of Mother Nature, the garden whispers, for they correspond with the cycles of your soul's growth. Quiet your mind. Rope in the restlessness. Be here. Learn to labour. Learn to wait. Learn to wait expectantly."

Sarah Ban Breathnach

Another source of profound pleasure and delight for nature-loving Taureans who've been overindulging in retail therapy is the simple pastime of gardening. The green love affair begins quietly at first. There is the innocent perusal of gardening catalogues, then the passion builds slowly through the planting of seeds in the seeming depths of midwinter, and then again as we watch excitedly for those first green shoots in spring.

Gardening has been described as one of the great rewards of middle age, but the joy of creating a garden – even if it's just a city window box – is one that can be experienced at any age. Gardening can also bring subtle, gradual financial benefits too. As a hobby, it teaches us how to wait, and to delay gratification, and we can apply this wisdom to the way we handle our finances. Learning how to do this is yet another stepping stone on the road to financial serenity.

"I am now willing to learn from the cycles of Nature."

♈ ♉ ♊ ♋ ♌ ♍ ♎ ♏ ♐ ♑ ♒ ♓

♊

Gemini

"In most undertakings, success requires not only initiative, but also finitiative!"

Anonymous

Culture

"Always leave enough time in your life to do something that makes you feel happy, satisfied, even joyous. That has more of an effect on economic well-being than any other single factor."

Paul Hawken

As Geminis, we have a certain basic requirement of our lives, namely that we have enough fun! We love entertainment in all its shapes and guises – movies, the theatre, concerts, the ballet, etc etc – and we need to make sure that we are feeding our essential need for culture. Sometimes, though, we can spend too much money indulging our love of the arts. If this is the case with you, you need to do some lateral thinking.

If you're broke, but love the cinema, why not get an evening job as an usher? Or simply wait for the latest releases to come out on video? If you start working as a volunteer for local radio and newspaper, you may qualify for free admission to many events, by getting yourself included on the Press List. If music is your love, volunteer to sell programmes at concerts. If you love paintings, get yourself invited to gallery previews.

Whatever your cultural "fix", there's always a low-cost way of enjoying it, if you are prepared to be patient and flexible.

"I now allow myself to enjoy my love of culture, whilst still living within my means."

Communication

"Money will come when you are doing the right thing."

Mike Phillips

With quick-witted Mercury as our planetary ruler, it's important that we understand the essential qualities we need in our work if we are to prosper. We want change, variety, and stimulation. We like to be entertained too, and we are never happier than when we are communicating. Do you feel your essential gifts lie in the field of speaking, writing, journalism or publishing? But have you shrunk from trying to develop a career in those areas, because you thought it was just too hard to even try?

The point to remember here is, if you don't go for what you really want to do, you are unlikely to prosper and you will doubtless spend far more money in the long run, attempting to cheer yourself up for your lack of fulfilment.

Start to develop your communication skills in a small way at first. Volunteer your services for free at the local newspaper or radio station, just to get started, and take it from there. You may be surprised at what follows.

"I am now willing to develop my natural talents and abilities."

Counting

"Often our spending differs from our real val-
ues. We fritter away cash on things we don't
cherish and deny ourselves those things we do.
For many of us, counting is a prelude to creative
luxury."

Julia Cameron

Would you like to try an exercise that will teach you more about your relationship with money than you ever dreamed possible? Buy yourself a small cash book, and just for one week, track all your spending meticulously. Write down everything you spend your money on – and on another page, write down all the money that you receive. Write down all the money you spend on magazines, food, utilities, clothes and your chosen entertainment, and everything else you buy. At the end of the week, analyse your spending. There it all is, in black and white.

When I first tried this simple practice, it had the magical effect of helping me cut back on those expenditures I suddenly saw were truly a waste of my money. In my case, the disaster zones were exorbitant bank charges and childcare fees. Where are your personal financial "black holes"? If you don't know this exercise will help you find out.

"I now keep track of every penny that I spend,
and every penny that I receive."

Faith

"Now is the time for women to break the barri-
ers of self-limitation. You can be far more than
you ever dreamed possible".

Louise Hay

If we are to move forward in the life we have chosen, we have to be conscious of the way we think about ourselves. There's an old saying, "As a man thinketh, so he is," and the truth of this axiom certainly applies to women too. Take your notebook, and write a list of the words you would use to describe yourself. "Witty, charming, capable, dynamic" are the kinds of words we would like to see on that list.

If your list is packed with negative adjectives, however, you need to ask yourself where those negative thoughts come from. Are these your own true beliefs about yourself, or are they simply things that were said to you in child-hood? You'll learn a technique for dealing with these "negatives" shortly – but meanwhile, focus on the positive beliefs you have about yourself. Look at your list often, and remind yourself you do have the ability to succeed.

"I now allow myself to think positive
thoughts about my life."

Affirmation

"The power of the word is real whether or not you are conscious of it. Your own words are the bricks and mortar of the dreams you want to realize. Behind every word flows energy."

Sonia Choquette

Affirmations are positive statements we can use to help create changes in our lives – and as such, they are so much more powerful than simple "positive thinking." Jerrold Mundis writes, "Affirmations ... are specific and powerful vehicles of change and if systematically employed, they can and do bring about such internal change, which by consequence leads to external change."

Affirmations are positive statements, rather like the Meditations you will find at the end of every page in this book. To create the most powerful personalised affirmations for you, take the negative adjectives that surfaced in your list of self-beliefs (see Faith) and re-frame them positively. For example, if you wrote, "I am impractical" or "I always spend too much money", you can reframe these beliefs as, "I am a practical woman", and "I now spend according to my means." Carry on rewriting all your "negatives" as positive statements, and say them to yourself each night before you go to sleep. Persevere with this, and you'll soon start to see dramatic changes in your life...

"I now use affirmations to create major shifts in my life."

Accountability

*"Many people take no care of their money until
they come nearly to the end of it, and others do
just the same with their time."*

Johann Wolfgang von Goethe

Once we understand the fundamental equation that
money does matter (because it equates to our life energy) –
and that how we spend it matters (because our spending
determines the emotional quality of our lives) we can
begin to understand the importance of being conscious of
how we spend our money.

Today, reflect on the things you've discovered you've been
spending your money on, through your practice of the
"Counting" Meditation. Do you really want and/or need
them? Do they really represent value for you, and an
appropriate use of your life energy? If not, start considering where you might like to make some changes in your
spending habits.

*"I am willing to be accountable for
all my spending."*

Responsibility

*"It may seem paradoxical, but what I am saying
is that our lives have become a hell not because
money is too important to us, but because, in a
certain sense, it is not important enough."*

Jacob Needleman

We Geminis have a kind of ambivalent attitude towards
financial responsibility; some days we feel like handling
money, other days we don't. We'd rather leave it to someone else. But being an adult does mean taking responsibility, for our money and our spending, and if there's a gap
twixt the two, taking steps to handle it!

How many times have we pushed a brown or white enve-
lope to the back of the drawer because we didn't want to
see how much money we owed on our taxes or on our
credit card bill? How many times did we "forget" to fill up
the car with petrol, or pay the electric bill, preferring to let
our spouse or partner take care of it? Denial is not a river
in Egypt, however, - so if you've been avoiding dealing
with money, resolve to make some changes...

**"I now take full responsibility for my
own finances."**

Conviviality

"The key to frugal entertaining and dating is to remember why you're doing it – to enjoy the company of other people. When you come right down to it, beyond a certain level of comfort, money doesn't make the encounter any more (or less) delightful. And the deepest levels of human connection have nothing to do with anything that money can buy."

Joe Dominguez and Vicki Robin

We Geminis are social creatures at heart, and we love to entertain – but sometimes our love of socializing can blow a major hole in our budget. The key to overcoming this is to surrender our attachment to being "the hostess with the mostest", and to adopt a more co-operative approach to entertaining.

If you want to have a dinner party, get your guests to bring dessert, and also something to drink. Or if you're catering for larger numbers, why not have a "pot-luck" supper where all the guests bring a contribution? With just a little forethought, it's easy to arrange who brings what, so that you don't get totally swamped with either salads or desserts. Plan your suppers and soirées around goods and items that are "on sale" or special offer, so as to maximise your budget.

"I now enjoy entertaining within my means."

Reconnaissance

"Money is like promises – easier made than kept."

Josh Billings

As Geminis, our mental powers and intellect are often our greatest financial assets, in many more ways than one. We can use our minds to help us earn our living, as salespeople and marketing experts, or as writers, journalists or broadcasters. But just as we can use our minds to earn money, we also need to use them to help us manage our money too…

Despite the mind-blowing complexity and volume of all the financial products on offer, we absolutely do have the ability to keep our finger on the pulse of what's new, and find deals that work best for us. We may protest to ourselves that this feels "boring" – but it's an investment of time that could yield rich dividends.

Time spent researching the array of financial products on offer can help us find a much cheaper mortgage deal, maximise the return on our savings, and avoid paying excess bank charges. Trawling the Sunday financial pages may in fact be all we need to do. Time far better spent than browsing the mall! Today, resolve to do the financial legwork you need to do, in order to get the best deals. It could well be your passport to financial serenity.

"I am now willing to spend quality time managing my finances."

Saving

"Save a part of your income and begin now, for the person with a surplus controls circumstances, and the person without a surplus is controlled by circumstances."

Henry H Buckley

We Geminis often dream of doing great things, like taking a year off work to write a novel, do an art course, or backpack around the globe – but unless we have the money to finance our dreams, they are in danger of remaining just dreams and no more. And generating a financial surplus isn't really such a difficult thing to do, given just a little planning and fiscal discipline.

Prosperity writers and commentators down the ages have recommended the practice of putting aside 10 per cent of your earnings in a "seed account" for future plans and projects. Carried out regularly, these savings will soon accumulate, thanks to the power of compound interest. Choose a high-interest savings account where withdrawals can only be made by giving a long period of notice. This will help guard against the possibility of your squandering your savings on impulse! And isn't it nice to think that you're helping to create your own financial freedom?

"I am now willing to save a part of all I earn."

Buried Treasure

"The ability to imagine is vital to all human progress. Just as all reforms and advances in civilization began with the imagination, so all improvement in your life begins with improved mental pictures."

Catherine Ponder

As Geminis, our ability to create a more prosperous future and start laying the foundations of financial serenity often lies in our willingness to use our mental powers in a constructive manner. Affirmations help us by using the spoken word. Treasure-mapping is another powerful way we can harness the power of thought and imagery.

Take your notebook and write a list of the goals you would like to achieve under the following headings: work, money, relationships, home, family, travel, creative projects, charitable work, etc. Then gather up a dozen or so glossy magazines. Every time you come to an image or picture that captures your attention and fits with one of your goals, cut it out.

Now take a larger piece of paper, and assemble all your images under your various headings. This is your treasure map. Keep it in clear view, and look at it often. This process imprints your goals on your unconscious mind more powerfully. If you wish, you can also amplify the process by writing your goals out as affirmations, and sticking them under the relevant sections of your treasure map.

"I now harness the power of creative imagery to help make my dreams come true."

Integrity

"If a person gets their attitude towards money straight, it will help straighten out almost every other area of their life."

Billy Graham

Mahatma Gandhi once said that honesty was incompatible with the amassing of a large fortune – and many of us would agree that perhaps he had a point. For when we are bent on making money, it's easy to twist the truth just a tad in the single-minded pursuit of our goals. And with our ruling planet, nimble-witted Mercury, influencing our financial activities, we frequently glimpse opportunities to turn affairs to our advantage and sometimes at the expense of others.

But if we are less than honest in our business dealings, it's we who will end up paying – because at the end of the day, we won't feel good about ourselves. Remember the Gemini media tycoon Robert Maxwell and the outrageously tangled web he wove?

The law of cause and effect spells out quite clearly that we WILL reap what we sow, and we are wise to remember it, especially where our finances are concerned. Even when we feel our backs are against the wall … there's never an excuse, really…

"I am a person of integrity in all my financial affairs."

♈ ♉ ♊ ♋ ♌ ♍ ♎ ♏ ♐ ♑ ♒ ♓

♋

Cancer

"Put not your trust in money, but put your money in trust."

Oliver Wendell Holmes

Lunar Wisdom

"Becoming attuned to the energies of the Moon and to our own intuitive lunar needs is essential if we seek to befriend ourselves and to create relationships which nourish and sustain ourselves and others."

Tracy Marks

As Cancerians, we are ruled by the Moon and thus are far more susceptible to its phases and phenomena than many other signs of the zodiac. The word "lunatic" is derived from the Latin word for Moon, "luna", and there's a traditional and well-documented link between the time of Full Moon in the heavens (and the few days prior, in the build-up to Full Moon), and our own increased tendency towards irrational behaviour. Yes, this is the time of the month when our spending may become very erratic, if not exactly crazy – that's if we don't commit crimes or howl at the Moon at midnight!

Seriously though, for Cancerians who are having trouble getting their finances under control, an understanding of how the Moon's cycle affects you is so, so important. Just chart your behaviour over a month or two and note how you feel (and spend) around both Full Moon and New Moon. Remember, forewarned is forearmed, so if you know you are likely to overspend at this time, you can take appropriate action! Like leaving your credit card and cheque book at home, for instance…

"I now take time to become aware of my personal cosmic rhythms."

Financial Serenity

"We're zealots at pursuing financial security when what we really hunger for is financial serenity. Financial serenity is never having to worry about money again because you've discovered the true Source... Financial serenity starts when we accept as our truth that money is a state of mind, and that abundance is a state of belief... When we choose abundance ... we attain true Wealth."

Sarah Ban Breathnach

Rather like the earth sign Taurus, we Cancerians can get very hung up on chasing that elusive phantom of Permanent Financial Security. But as a very good friend of mine once pointed out, striving after security is really like seeking the unattainable, since we're never totally in possession of all the facts. For we can never, ever truly know the future, in spite of all our planning. For example, once you've made your pile, who's to say (heaven forbid) that you won't then succumb to a life-threatening disease?...

So the best approach of all is to cultivate an attitude of financial serenity – the serendipitous art of being grateful for all that you do have. For it's a universal law that people who regularly say "Thank You" for what they have, tend to receive even more!

"I now understand that all I have is all I need."

Emotional Equilibrium

*"It's terribly amusing how many different cli-
mates of feeling one can go through in a day."*
Anne Morrow Lindbergh

We Cancerians certainly know a thing or two about feelings. In fact, I'd say we're master artists of the palette of
emotional shades, hues and timbres – as anyone who has
lived or worked with us can verify! Our day can start out
sunny, mood-wise, but stir in a little squall with the boss or
our workmates, and the weather can soon get pretty
stormy...

But what do my feelings have to do with my finances? I
hear you ask. The short answer is – everything. Why?
Because people who are constantly upset tend to make bad
financial decisions. In addition, Cancerians can also be
particularly prone to that tricky little habit of binge spending, squandering money a-plenty when they feel they're in
need of "cheering up"...

So what helps? Stressbusting, centring practices like meditation and yoga can soothe your emotions and help you
feel less volatile. So can swimming, taking walks in nature,
or simply sitting in a park or garden. Try one of these techniques next time you feel mad, anxious or blue. Chances
are, you will feel much calmer before long. And your bank
balance won't have suffered in the meantime either...

**"I now commit myself to the path of
inner peace."**

Release

"When you forgive and let go, not only does a huge weight drop off your shoulders, but the doorway to your own self-love opens."

Louise Hay

We Cancerians have a well-developed sense of self-preservation – it's something to do with that crustaceous shell of ours. But like all water signs, we tend to take life very personally, and are quick to take offence.

If you feel that someone has done you a bad turn, however, it's unwise (but very easy) to harbour grudges and resentments. The very best course of action really is to let it go – because otherwise, you are simply squandering your valuable life energy getting caught up in petty quarrels and disputes.

If you have a daily "quiet time" or meditation period, make a point of reviewing the day's events and reconsidering whatever it is that you maybe need to let go of. You'll have far more energy left over for carrying out the real business of your life – whatever that happens to be…

"I am now willing to forgive."

Courage

"Life shrinks or expands in proportion to one's courage."

Anais Nin

Life is a bit like the running-shoe advert – we really do need to "just do it" – but we crabs get so cautious and nervous that we often find it hard to pursue our own dreams and visions.

One inner technique that Stephen "Seven Habits" Covey recommends is that of fast-forwarding to your own funeral. What are those things that you would really love to do before you leave the planet? Make a list of them – it could be anything from travelling round the world to learning to dance the tango! Look at your list – are you taking steps to make any of those things happen? If not, why not?

Promise yourself that today you will really start to live the life you want. Take baby steps. These baby steps will lead you towards the life you want to lead, and away from dysfunctional spending, and its resultant prison of debt.

"I now allow myself to move towards the life I truly desire."

Self Nurturing

"I'd rather have roses on my table than diamonds round my neck."

Emma Goldman

In zodiac mythology, Cancer is the sign of the Great Mother, and the sign of Cancer has a great deal to do with mothering and nurturing. Statistics show that a prodigious number of caring crabs work in the helping professions, and we excel at taking care of others, and making them feel good about themselves.

But how often do we take the time to treat ourselves as kindly as we treat others? Today, take a few minutes to reflect on what it is that gives you a real sense of comfort in your life. Is it fresh flowers on your dining table, as it was for Ms Goldman? Or do you draw sustenance from a fragrantly scented bubble bath, or a delicious home-cooked meal, lovingly prepared by your significant other? Look around your home, and do a quick "comfort audit".... Do your surroundings truly nurture you? Is there enough of your favourite food in the refrigerator, and are there enough comfy cushions on the sofa? If not, why not? Think what you can do to make your life more comfortable, and promise yourself you will make a start today.

"I now love and take care of myself."

Understanding

"Although we are largely unconscious of our own financial belief systems, our blindness condemns us to prisons of our own making."

J Blyth

The Moon, Cancer's planetary ruler, has a great deal to do with unconscious behaviour and habit patterns – those ways of dealing with life (and money) that we learned at our mother's knee. Today, allow yourself some time to consider what the financial atmosphere was like in the home you grew up in. Did you feel that life was abundant, and that there was always enough money for everyone's needs – or were you given the message that money came hand in hand with struggle, and that there was always "too much month at the end of the money?"

Were your family spenders or savers? Did your parents share the task of dealing with the family finances, or did one parent handle all the money solo? Were major purchases and financial decisions taken as a family, or did your mother or father spend in secret?

What about debt? Did you grow up observing that it was "normal" to live on an overdraft and credit cards, or did your parents live within their means? You are influenced by all this early conditioning around money far more than you may know. Decide today whether you're going to handle money the same way your parents did – or whether you would like to be different... Remember, identifying early patterns is the first step to changing them.

"I now allow myself to choose my own financial beliefs."

Honouring the Ancestors

"Remembering the past gives power to the present."

Fae Myenne Ng

Our experience of growing up in a family, however small or fragmented that family was, endows us with many intangible blessings, in addition to any financial inheritance we may receive. All too often, we in the West have lost our links with tradition, but taking time to reflect on our family heritage can often be a great source of comfort and strength. Remembering the trials and difficulties our grandparents survived can act as "soul food" for us, and also help put our own daily challenges into a wider perspective…

Today, make time to arrange a visit to your family elders if this is possible and practical. If not, spend time looking through the family photograph albums. Think about the qualities you've inherited from your grandparents – grandma's intuition, perhaps, or your granddad's strength and perseverance. Remember, and give thanks.

The unseen web of Family is a great source of support to most Cancerians. Sometimes, it's only when we remember where we've really come from that we can truly discover where we're going…

"I now take time to honour my ancestors."

Attunement

"All you need is deep within you waiting to unfold and reveal itself. All you have to do is to be still and take time to seek for what is within, and you will surely find it."

Eileen Caddy

As Cancerians, one of our most valuable assets is our intuition, that inner voice or sense of knowing that pierces the veil of rationality and cuts right to the chase. It's the "sixth sense" that tells you the right foods to eat, the right college course to take, and the right man to marry. Intuition is a gift from God, and we need to see it as such. Follow it faithfully, and the river of life will flow smoothly without stopping. Go against it, and you'll be amazed at how soon you end up capsizing in the rapids.

My dear friend Ellen Hayakawa tells wonderful stories about how her inner intuitive Voice – which she understands to be the voice of God - functions in her life. One day, the Voice told her to fly back home to Canada before returning to her next conference date, involving an extra $600 worth of expenditure on air fares. Ellen was reluctant at first, but she obeyed the Voice. The day after returning home she received a phone call asking her to be a keynote speaker at a major conference, alongside Deepak Chopra. Had she not followed her Voice, the opportunity would have been missed. Instead, her career as a speaker took a quantum leap forward!

As Cancerians gifted with excellent powers of attunement, our challenge is to listen to our own inner voice - and to find the courage to follow it...

"I now listen to and act on my intuition."

Clearing

"Before you let anything into your life, you have to let something go ... when energy can't flow easily, it stagnates. Clutter creates stagnation and makes everything grind to a halt, it makes you feel depressed, tired and stuck."

Sarah Shurety

We Cancerians we can sometimes get into heavy denial about our tendency to spend too much, and we also love to hang on to the fruits of our retail therapy. We try vainly to disguise our habit by calling it "collecting" – but the bottom line is, our homes very often contain far more stuff than we'll ever need or use.

Since prosperity and abundance truly cannot flow into a cluttered space, clearing out unwanted items does need to be a high priority. If getting rid of your junk feels like Mission Impossible, why not hold a garage sale and donate the proceeds to your favourite children's' charity?

Your rule of thumb for clearing out should be, if you haven't used anything within the last year, get rid of it. Broken stuff should be junked too, if you don't think you're going to get round to mending it. Enlist a friend to help you sort items, if you feel this task is beyond you. And banish the phrase "it might come in useful" from your vocabulary. I promise you, it won't...

"I now release unwanted possessions from my life."

Trust

"Trust that the Universe is working WITH you and FOR you."

Sanaya Roman

As security-minded Cancerians, it's easy for us to fall into the trap of making so much provision for the future that we almost forget to live in the present. But it's important to remember that since we are ruled by the Moon, all things (including money) will tend to "come and go" in our lives.

To really understand how this works, it helps to spend time – several hours, preferably – sitting on the seashore, watching the ebb and flow of the tide. Water comes in, water flows out. Money comes in, money flows out. We may not have much money at the moment, but abundance will return to us, provided we continue to practise thinking and acting in an abundant manner.

We need to learn to trust that the money will be there when we need it, put our worries and concerns to one side, and carry on working at the work that we feel we are meant to be doing in this life. Just trust...

"I trust in the process of life. I am safe."

Home Truths

"Don't lose sight of the fact that the purchase price is only part of the cost of a new home... Indeed, you can be sure that for as long as you own a home you will be paying for SOME-THING – new furniture, old boiler, leaky pipes – at all times."

Alvin Hall

As Cancerians, it's very important for us to feel we have a secure base, a solid foundation in life, and more often than not, this base is our home. We are hugely attached to it, and given the choice, many Cancerians would simply never leave it! For many crabs, bricks and mortar provide emotional anchoring as well as financial security, and we love to spend lavishly on our homes.

Whilst establishing our Cancerian haven can be a delightful, fun thing to do, we may need to guard against the tendency to get caught up in our fantasies of the "ideal home", and the overspending that this may entail. Financial guru Alvin Hall recently hosted a TV money makeover show which featured one young couple who had run up debts of around $42,000 making their new home look picture perfect. Then the husband lost his job, and the newlyweds suffered many sleepless nights worrying how they were going to pay off the debt. Remember, the ideal home is one we can easily afford – not one that costs so much that it totally drains and exhausts us.

"I now spend wisely on creating a home that truly sustains me."

♈ ♉ ♊ ♋ ♌ ♍ ♎ ♏ ♐ ♑ ♒ ♓

♌

Leo

*"I don't know much about being a millionaire,
but I bet I'd be darling at it."*

Dorothy Parker

Luxury

*"It's possible to own too much. A woman with
one watch knows what time it is; a woman with
two watches is never quite sure."*

Lee Segall

Asking a Leo to give up their love of luxury would be a seriously cruel thing to do, and I wouldn't dream of suggesting
it, for all Leos know they were born to enjoy the very best in
life. But what can be done when our bank balance doesn't
live up to our aspirations, and our luxurious longings look
set to plunge us deep into debt? The trick here is to master
the art of sustainable luxury, and to allow ourselves "a little
of what we fancy"… this ensures that we carry on feeling
good, and our bank balance stays in the black.

How do we practise the art of sustainable luxury? By buying a single red rose for our lover, instead of a massive bou-
quet; by treating ourselves to a cashmere scarf instead of a
cashmere twinset; by going for cocktails or coffee at the
best hotel in town, rather than a full five-course banquet
that neither our finances nor our waistline can truly afford;
or by buying all the ingredients for a truly gourmet feast,
and preparing it at home for a fraction of the cost. The idea
is to allow yourself to have a taste of what you want, without totally blowing your budget.

The truth is, luxury can be totally accessible and affordable
if you just re-think it a little, no matter how limited your
resources…

"I now allow myself to enjoy the very best in life."

Sufficiency

"I'm living so far beyond my income that we may almost be said to be living apart."

e e cummings

As the "royal" sign of the zodiac, we Leos hate the idea of placing limits on our spending – but the fact of the matter is, if we don't do it for ourselves, someone else will do it for us – most likely the bank manager, when they call in our overdraft or loan! So it's best to take a little financial medicine now, rather than a whole lot later.

Follow the Counting meditation (see Gemini) and write down all your spending for at least one week. Log your income at the same time. Is there a small gap twixt the two? Or does that gap look more like the Grand Canyon? If so, you need to start looking at ways you can cut back on expenses. But don't panic – this book contains dozens of ideas for living well on less, so just keep reading. But if you're living on an ever-expanding overdraft, you do need to acknowledge that you do have a problem, and that you need to adjust your lifestyle.

"I now commit myself to controlling my spending behaviour."

Self-Expression

"Ironically, when we give ourselves, by our own hand, the dignity we crave, and the right to support and validate our own work, so many locked doors mysteriously open!"

Julia Cameron

We Leos are renowned collectors of fine art, or amazing handcrafted jewellery and silk, and those stunning, totally unique ceramic pieces that grace the pedestals and plinths of the very best galleries in town. We adore all that's exquisite and totally individual. We are the great collectors of the "one-off" and financing our aesthetic sensibilities and good taste can play havoc with our bank balance.

But if we look a little deeper, we could just see that the real reason we love all this stuff is that we long to make art ourselves. Leo is ruled by the Sun, the sign of creativity, and the lion that isn't busy creating, is usually busy buying in the ready-mades instead!

Today, commit yourself to exploring your creative potential – even if you feel you lack talent, or that you simply haven't got the time...

"I now commit myself to exploring my true creative potential."

Joy

"Follow your bliss."

Joseph Campbell

Now that we have committed ourselves to the process of exploring our creativity, we need to focus in on the precise form that our creative impulses would most like to take.

What will do it for you? Is it painting, sculpting or playing the piano? Would you like to throw terracotta pots or paint them, or learn contemporary dance, before you feel it's too late?   It's never too late, by the way…

Do your creative urges express themselves best in the kitchen or the printmaking studio? If you're stumped for inspiration, look back to when you were a child. What did you love doing most back then? What is it you really love to do most? Go do it.

"I now allow myself to do what I love most in life."

Ingenuity

"Perfection consists not in doing extraordinary things, but in doing ordinary things extraordinarily well."

Angelique Arnauld

As Leos, we always want life to be extraordinary – we want to throw the most amazing parties and have the most wonderful careers, whilst all the while wearing the most stunning outfits! But the art of making our lives truly wonderful and magical does not depend on the amount of money we throw at our lives each day, but on the attention we bring to even the simplest things that we do.

A meal cooked at home and served at a table that has been dressed with love and care can taste finer than dinner at Maxim's. Trust me on this. And there's always an ingenious way of living well on a budget if we look for it. Turn your dining room into a "restaurant at home" if you're cutting back on eating out for a while. If you can't afford an expensive package holiday, consider house swapping instead. Start a baby-sitting swap circle among friends, instead of paying for sitters when you go out, and so on…

"I now discover ingenious ways of making the most of my resources."

Elegance

"I discovered that when it comes with clothes – as with many other things – less is definitely more. It's so much simpler to work with a few classic pieces that are always in style, and work with each other than to have a closet jammed with all the latest fashions that don't look good for long, and seldom work together."

Elaine St James

As the quintessential "royal" sign of the zodiac, we Leo women always want to look our best – but if you look at the wealthiest women in the world, you'll find they nearly always plump for classic looks in timeless styles and colours. Maybe it's a good time to take a ruthless look at your wardrobe, and weed out the "junk" fashions to make room for an elegant capsule wardrobe that really works for you. Get advice on your "best look" from a department store or personal shopper, if needs be. After all, isn't it better to have one superb outfit that you look and feel totally stunning in, than three cheaper high-fashion get-ups that will only be fit for Goodwill at the end of the season?

Other money-saving clothes tips: limit your clothes buying to the start of the season or better still, Sale time… Trade outfits with a girlfriend who's the same size as you. Put away outfits you no longer like wearing and "trade" clothes with yourself in the future.

"I now allow myself to dress with true elegance."

Setting the Stage

"We shape our dwellings, and afterwards, our dwellings shape us."

Sir Winston Churchill

We Leo women are justly renowned for our sense of high drama and theatrical style – and nowhere is this more apparent than in the way we decorate our homes. Leo houses and apartments are often decked out in eye-catching shades of fiery red and gold, or vibrant jewel shades of royal, emerald and mauve. We always want our surroundings to look great, so we do need to learn how to decorate for maximum effect on a minimal budget.

Shortcuts to cut-price opulence including buying paint, fabrics and soft furnishings on sale, and learning to shop wisely at auctions and estate sales, which often have great antiques and pieces of furniture at knockdown prices (take a friend, and tell them not to let you bid over the odds!). Learn to paint, wallpaper and upholster at evening classes, instead of hiring in decorators – it's thrifty and can also be great fun! When you've made your home look totally stunning, you can consider hiring it out as a film set location. Why not let your house really earn its keep, and become a movie star?!

"I now create the right surroundings at the right price."

Play

"Skill is not the answer, nor is money. What you need is optimism, humanism, enthusiasm, intuition, curiosity, love, humour, magic and fun, and that secret ingredient – euphoria!"

Anita Roddick

Since Leo is the sign of the child, it's vital to our sense of happiness and wellbeing that we make time to play and have enough fun in our lives. The link between humour and health is well proven, and since laughter keeps us hale and hearty, we need to make it a top priority.

Make a commitment with yourself to have a Fun Date each week, and be sure to stick to it, however busy your schedule. It could be something as simple as renting a video that features your favourite comedian, and making huge buckets of popcorn to eat while you watch it. Or inviting round some girlfriends with a known talent for making you laugh. Remember, you don't necessarily have to spend money – the important thing is just to do something that makes you laugh!

"I now allow myself to have fun every week."

Receptivity

"Listening is a form of accepting."

Stella Terrill Mann

As Leos, we always think that we know best about every-thing – but although we make great business managers, managing our own finances is not always our strongest forte. Shirley Conran, bestselling author of "Down with Superwoman" has got this one right, I think. She said, "Know what you're good at and do it, and know what you're not good at, and don't do it!"

So, if the facts of your financial situation tend to suggest that you're not the world's greatest financial manager, it's time to get some help. Ask around amongst your friends, and find a good financial adviser you can really trust. Employ an accountant you feel you can really talk to. And then make a point of really listening to their advice, and start putting it into practice. It's hard, I know, but there really are some people out there who may be able to give you some really great advice. I just hope you'll take it!

"I am now willing to listen to the expert opinion of others."

Recovery

"Debtors Anonymous says we go into debt to avoid feelings, especially feelings of deprivation (like other addictions, debt allows us to deny pain, sorrow, loss, anger and despair). Is your tendency to use your credit card simply a habit, or is it an addiction?"

Joe Dominguez and Vicki Robin

The sign of Leo is also the sign of the child, and for many of us, the roots of our spending disorders are buried deep in childhood. For some of us, splashing out on designer outfits is a desperate ploy to attract the attention and approval we did not get as children. Or if we felt unloved, we may now try to buy friendship by showering friends and family with inappropriately costly gifts.

Today, take time out to really check in with yourself about your spending, and why you do what it is that you do. It's not always possible for us to unravel old wounds ourselves, so you also might want to consider working on your spending issues in therapy. If your spending is a symptom of a deeper malaise, you need to understand that the situation isn't going to improve until you commit yourself to dealing with the cause.

"I now commit myself to healing the wounds of the past."

Judgement

"I knew that I had to win ... it did not occur to me then that every man in the room held the same conviction. What gambler ever thinks he's going to lose?"

Lisa St Aubin de Teran (from The Palace)

We Leos love to take risks, and putting it bluntly, many of us have a gambling problem. Oh, but I've never even been to Las Vegas, I hear you say, what can she be talking about? But gambling isn't just about playing the tables, or betting too much at poker, by any means.

In our everyday lives, we gamble when we take unwise risks, and put our financial well being on the line. We are gambling when we put our house up for collateral and start our own business without being sufficiently clued-up about what we are doing. We are gambling when we take on the wrong business partner, and leave them in charge of the cheque book. We are gambling when we pay off our boyfriend's credit card bill, when we know he'll just run it up again. We are gambling when we open a joint account with our lover, although we have a sneaky feeling that we shouldn't.

We know when we are gambling. So let's allow ourselves to take only the wisest of risks from now on...

"I now allow myself to exercise good judgement in all my financial dealings."

Generosity

"The wise and moral person shines like a fire on a hilltop, making money like the bee which does not hurt the flower. Such a person makes their pile as an anthill, gradually. People grown wealthy thus can help their family and firmly bind their friends to themselves."

Buddhist saying

As Leos, our generosity is one of the virtues that makes us shine, and no-one, but no-one, has deeper pockets than ours. We adore helping out our loved ones when they've run into problems, and we get a warm, inner glow when someone comes to us for a loan and we are able to oblige them. Of course, most of the time we don't really like to ask for it back. They might think we were being mean, or that we're broke or something. God forbid. And as for giving presents! Well, we love holiday time, because it's a chance to really show what we're made of, isn't it? We love giving presents, because we like to make other people happy.

There is absolutely nothing wrong with any of this – but one of the great lessons for Leos is to learn to give only what they can truly afford. Don't fall into the trap of borrowing money to lend it to other people. And if you can't afford to give a cashmere sweater, give a cashmere scarf instead...

"I now allow myself to give only what I can truly afford to give."

♈ ♉ ♊ ♋ ♌ ♍ ♎ ♏ ♐ ♑ ♒ ♓

♍

Virgo

*"Your work is to discover your work
and then with all your heart to give
yourself to it."*

Buddha

Clear Vision

*"We have first raised a dust and then complain
we cannot see."*

Bishop George Berkeley

Every Virgo woman longs to really live up to her image as
the Ms Efficiency of the zodiac, but that longed-for idyll of
total order in our domestic and financial affairs so often
seems to elude us. But why should this be so, when we
clearly have such a talent for organizing?

The answer often lies in a lack of clear vision: all too often,
we allow ourselves to get totally bogged down in the
details of our everyday lives, and then can't see the wood
for the trees. We have lost our vision, our clarity and our
sense of direction. We may also get sidetracked by unnec-
essary expenditures for life goals that are no longer relevant...

Today, take your notebook, and write out the two or three
major goals that sum up your sense of what your life is all
about – in other words, your vision. While you're about it,
also write two or three steps you can take today to make
your vision happen.

Do this every day for a week. It helps.

**"I now have a clear vision of my
life's direction."**

Order

"If you just get rid of the clutter, you never have to organize it."

Elaine St James

In a kind of parallel mirroring of the mental clutter that often clouds our minds and make us prey to worry and fretfulness, we Virgos often surround ourselves with a host of superfluous objects and clutter. I once knew an old Virgo couple who lived in a house that was so cluttered it was almost impossible to move around from room to room. Remembering times of shortage during World War II, they never threw anything away "in case it came in useful" – but once an object disappeared into the ocean of junk that surrounded them, it was almost impossible to retrieve it. So they'd then have to go out and buy another comb, hairbrush, tube of face-cream, or whatever … thus adding even more to the mountain of clutter.

Clutter wastes our time (looking for things), it wastes our energy (maintaining and organising things) and it also wastes our money (when we need to replace an item because we cannot find the original!).

Today, resolve to free yourself of clutter. It won't happen overnight – but promise you'll make a start … start with one room, one drawer, one box of junk … and then continue each day until you have freed yourself of clutter.

"I now surround myself only with objects that I want and need."

Self-Love

"A woman cannot be comfortable without her own approval."

Mark Twain

As Virgos, we often suffer from a kind of false modesty about our true worth that can lead us to treat ourselves less than kindly. How many times have we been guilty of hurling compliments back at the donor with an expression of self-loathing? "You like my dress? Oh, this old thing, I got it from the thrift shop!" "You like my hair? I just got it done – Oh, I don't know, I'm not sure if it suits me…"

Learning to like ourselves more is an essential step on the road to financial serenity and abundance, because being at peace with ourselves is a necessary prelude to feeling at peace around money.

Today, take your notebook and start a Self-Love section. Jump-start the process by writing out twenty things that you like about yourself. Each night before you go to sleep, write out three things you liked about yourself today. Read both lists each night before retiring. As you focus on the positive things about yourself, your life will slowly but surely begin to improve. All you have to do is start – and continue!

"I now like and approve of myself."

Magical Thinking

*"The thoughts we choose to think are the tools
we use to paint the canvas of our lives."*

Louise Hay

The link between our thoughts and the events that take place in our lives has been known and understood since ancient times – as evidenced by the following sayings: "as a man (or woman) thinketh, so he (she) is", "thoughts are things", and "you are what you think".

Since we Virgos often have a truly Olympian capacity for worry and negative thinking, we need to make a special point of monitoring our thoughts, and making sure that they are positive.

If you don't have a quiet time each day, start to create one. Use these precious minutes to start thinking more positively about your life, and form images and pictures of how you would like your life to be. These images can relate to any aspect of your life that you would like to change. The magic thing about this process is that it's limitless – and if you continue with this visualizing practice on a daily basis, you will soon discover for yourself how your thoughts can help you start to create the life you want…

**"I now allow myself to think positively about
my life at all times."**

Self Esteem

"To love oneself is the beginning of a lifelong romance."

Oscar Wilde

Once we Virgos have mastered the first steps towards liking ourselves, we can move on to the greater challenge of loving ourselves – unconditionally! Wow, what a prospect!

Back in my twenties, I once shared a house with a filmmaker friend who was totally brilliant at loving herself. When her boyfriend dumped her for another woman, she treated herself gently – wore her favourite clothes, went out for gentle drinks and dinners with caring friends, took long, hot scented baths and organised the extra-special vacation she'd been dreaming of for ages. Would that we all treated ourselves so kindly!

Today, think about how you can love yourself more, regardless of your circumstances. Take yourself out on a date to somewhere you've been longing to go; buy yourself a bunch of flowers; have a quiet, candlelit evening at home, listening to your favourite music. Be nice to yourself. After all it's the one love affair that could last the rest of your life…

"I am now willing to love myself unconditionally!"

Contentment

"Heaven on earth is a choice I can make rather than a place I must find."

Dr Wayne W Dyer

As the wise Virgins of the zodiac, we have a yen for perfection. We are always striving to do better in our work, to achieve higher standards of tidiness and cleanliness in our homes, etc, etc. But this constant striving for perfection doesn't always make us easy to live with. Yearning for perfection can also keep us in a kind of materialistic trap of continually wanting more and better consumer items, as what was once "perfect" and "state of the art" gradually becomes outmoded.

Today, I would like you to take some time to reflect on how great your life already is, just as it is in the present moment. Gratitude and appreciation for what you already are and have are essential to this step. Cultivating an inner sense of contentment with your life is the key that can help you escape from that restless state of craving, into a feeling of serenity and peace...

"I am now content with my life, exactly as it is."

Downshifting

"Once you simplify your life, you can start, per-haps all over again, to live your best life, what-ever that is for you."

Anne Morrow Lindbergh

Downshifting is a variation on the theme of simplicity, and we Virgos often find that we start to downshift naturally when we begin to free ourselves of all the clutter and junk that we've accumulated over the years.

When I did my first major "de-junking" of my house – at that time, a country cottage in Wiltshire – an irrepressible feeling of freedom came over me. By the time I had finished, I realized we no longer needed such a large house (or such a large mortgage) since we no longer had so much junk! By spending less and simplifying our financial commitments and living arrangements - in other words, down-shifting - my husband and I could free up more time to do what we loved, and get in touch with our true life purpose.

Do you have a financial commitment that is stopping you from "living your best life?" Can you change it? If so, how?

"I now allow myself to simplify my life."

Service

"A man's true wealth is the good he does in the world."

Mohamed

We Virgos love nothing more in life than to be useful, and no Virgo will be happy on this planet until they have truly found a way to serve. But what does it mean to serve? It means to find that place in life where we know we can do something to help.

We can find a way to serve right in the heart of our own family – such as teaching your own child to read, or looking after an elderly relative. Or the urge to serve could lead us further out into society, to that place where we perceive the most urgent need, and know we can do something about it.

Today, take a few moments to consider where you feel drawn to serve. Where is your passion? Do you want to help the homeless, the terminally sick? Do you want to work with children or the mentally ill? Or do you simply want to make time to help more people within your own circle of acquaintance? Whatever it is, commit yourself to finding the time to do it...

"I now enjoy helping others in my life."

Right Livelihood

"Doing things right is not as important as doing the right things."

Anonymous

Once we have come to grips with our perfectionist tendencies, and acknowledged our need to serve in some way, we are well on the way to earning our living in the "right" way – and thus taking another step on the road to financial serenity. For money is always less of a problem when we are doing the right thing...

So what is the "right thing" for you? Do you have a sense of vocation about your work? If not, why not? Are you doing work that you love? If not, why not? If you feel that you are trapped in a job you hate, "just to pay the bills", your financial situation is unlikely to improve until you resolve to make some changes. Changes that will take you in the direction of doing what you love – every single day of your life.

"I now commit myself to doing what I love for a living."

The Art of The Small

"It was the little things, taken one by one and savoured, that made it all worthwhile."

Rumer Godden

Little things mean a lot to Virgo, and in order to find true serenity in life, financial and otherwise, we need to take time to notice life's details. It's said that Taureans always take time to sniff the roses on the way to the bank, and we Virgos also need to make sure that our "busyness" doesn't rob us of the everyday joys of living.

Those little things like taking time to make our own greetings cards, or even a little gift for a loved one's birthday, instead of a hectic last-minute dash to the mall. The smell of clean laundry … the mouth-watering aroma of spaghetti sauce simmering on the stove … baking home-made biscuits to surprise someone special … watching a child sleep. What are the little things that really "make your day"? Have you taken time to do at least two of them today? Promise yourself that you will … today, and every day. Remember, God is in the details.

"I now take time every day to enjoy the details of my life"

Anticipation

"Your attitude determines your experience of the world."

Sanaya Roman

We Virgos can sometimes be the all-time champion worriers of the zodiac. Sound familiar? We need to learn to check this tendency within ourselves, and to see it for what it is – negative thinking. So, if you like to think of yourself as a positive person, but spend a significant time in worrying, you are actually undermining your own best efforts…

Neuro-Linguistic Programming guru Anthony Robbins exhorts us to "drive the car in the direction we want to go" – and we need to learn to re-frame our worrying into inner images and messages of positive expectancy instead. So, next time you find yourself thinking about What Could Possibly Go Wrong, make yourself stop – and then take a few seconds to cancel out the negative image and visualise things working out just fine instead … you'll find it soon becomes a habit!

"I now commit myself to thinking positively about my life at all times."

Joyous Routine

"How we spend our days is, of course, how we spend our lives."

Annie Dillard

Although we Virgos are by no means fixed in our nature, we flourish best when we understand our own daily rhythm and stick to a familiar routine. This routine extends to knowing what are the best foods for us to eat, the best time of the day to eat them, how much sleep we need, how much exercise we need to take, and the best way to take it. Etcetera, etcetera …

Having a set day of the week when we tidy and clean our house thoroughly, sort papers, and deal with our financial paperwork is also helpful and conducive to our sense of inner wellbeing.

We also need to make time in our routine for the things that really bring us pleasure just for their own sake – in less stressful, hurried times, these things used to be called hobbies! Do you have a favourite handicraft or pastime that you love to practise, but seldom allow yourself to? Is it tapestry, crochet or hooking rugs – or do you love to play the piano, or doodle with pastels? Many a successful business story started out as a homespun hobby – so indulge in your passion today, and make it part of your joyous routine.

"I now enjoy discovering the daily routine that works best for me."

♈ ♉ ♊ ♋ ♌ ♍ ♎ ♏ ♐ ♑ ♒ ♓

♎

Libra

"I'm giving you a definite maybe."

Sam Goldwyn

Independence

"You have to be to share, yet you have to share to be."

Jet Izabella Thurman

With pleasure-loving Venus as our ruling planet, we Librans often have a tendency to want to delegate all financial matters to our partner. But in this age of soaring divorce rates, no woman can afford to be financially co-dependent. Financial independence isn't just about earning your own money; it's about taking responsibility for looking after it too. We are blessed with fine Libran minds to help us research the best financial products for our needs – so let's use them, shall we?

Few things in life matter more to a Libran woman than her marriage or partnership, but we must not lose sight of the fact that in order to share life fully, we must first have a Self to bring to the relationship. And the ability to handle money wisely is a desirable attribute for that Self to possess...

Today, take a long, cool look at your financial arrangements, and be honest with yourself. Are you delegating too much financial responsibility to others? If so, promise yourself that you'll start to make some changes. Where money's concerned, don't let "sharing" become "not caring".

"I now commit myself to taking care of my own finances."

Aesthetics

"People with a strong Libran emphasis in their chart just seem to have a knack, a way of making their surroundings look beautiful, even on the most limited budget. With just the right shade of paint, or a simple colourful throw or cushion, they can totally transform a room. It's amazing how they do it."

Hugh Benson

There's no denying it, we Libran women have just got bags of style, and we know how to use it. One of the challenges of healing our finances, and attaining financial serenity, is that of making our homes look attractive and tasteful without sending our credit card balance zooming into the stratosphere.

What tools and techniques can you master that will help you to achieve this goal? Perhaps you'd like to learn special painting finishes that will help you avoid using expensive wallpaper; or create lavish drapes by using lengths of budget-priced calico; or pick up great furniture at auction for a fraction of the retail cost; or use a discount shopping guide to source top products at knockdown prices – and so on. If you're a homeowner, your decorating skills can add value to your property too. And who knows? One day you might even end up being asked to design other people's interiors. Many, many Librans have built profitable careers just through having good taste...

"I now surround myself with affordable style and beauty."

Feng Shui

"Although we all have our own separate fields of energy, we are all linked together, and everything around us, animate and inanimate, has an influence. Feng Shui's aim is to balance all these energies to ensure we are harmoniously in accord with the universe."

Sarah Shurety

The ancient art of Feng Shui is based on the guiding principle that since all of life is interrelated, the various areas of our homes correspond to the various areas of our lives. According to the bagua, the nine-sector template that is the cornerstone of Feng Shui philosophy, these are: the journey, helpful friends, creativity, relationships, illumination, fortunate blessings, the ancestors and health. When one of these areas of our home is blocked or "missing", we may suffer difficulties in the corresponding areas of our lives.

There are various "cures" that can be effected to remedy such shortcomings, and many, many books that you can read about Feng Shui to help you apply its wisdom. If you're feeling "stuck" or stagnant, however, there are two easy ways to get your life moving again. First, clear out all clutter – that's a basic requirement. Then, move twenty-seven objects in your home that haven't been moved in a year. You may feel sceptical about this, but try just try it anyway. It works!

"I now strive to bring all the areas of my life into balance."

Partnership

"Who would you take to the war with you?"

Julia Cameron

With Libra as our birth sign, we are ruled by Venus, the goddess of Love, and few things are more important to us on this earth than feeling cosily tucked up in a satisfying relationship. Unfortunately, our Libran need to be constantly coupled can be so totally all-consuming that we often get into the wrong relationship, or stay in a bad one, simply because of this blind, irrational need to be part of a couple.

But the fact is, IF a relationship does not truly support you, it isn't worth having. You may find yourself betraying the fact that you're unhappy by eating too many sweet foods, or buying too many clothes – or by drinking, overspending, or some other toxic habit.

Today, take a long, cool look at your relationship. Does your partner share life's burdens equally with you? Do they support your goals and most cherished dreams and ambitions? Or do they subtly (or not so subtly) undermine the goals you are trying to achieve? Be honest … the answers may surprise you.

"I now commit myself to building truly healthy relationships with others."

Resourcefulness

"When there is a lack of resourcefulness, inventiveness and innovation, thrift means doing without. When creativity combines with thrift, you may be doing without money, but you are not doing without."

Amy Dacyczyn

Libra is an air sign, so when we Librans are faced with a problem, we strive to fix it by using our minds. This can be a great asset when we're struggling to bring our spending under control, because we can use that dazzling intellect of ours to dream up all sorts of alternatives to spending money we don't really have.

Today, if you're facing a cash-flow crunch, or simply need to cut back on expenses, take some time to think up ways of gaining the essence of what you want without digging yourself deeper into debt. For example, if you've realised you're spending too much money on eating out, you could copy the Leo trick and create a "restaurant at home"; when you need a ball-gown, hire one instead of buying one; buy your air tickets well ahead of time, and scout around for the very best deals; make gifts and cards for loved ones - and so on. You can always come up with a low-cost alternative to store-bought items if you think and plan sufficiently far ahead.

"I now connect with my inner resourcefulness."

Beauty

"If of thy mortal goods thou art bereft,
And from thy slender store
Two loaves alone to thee are left,
Sell one, and with the dole
Buy hyacinths to feed thy soul!"

Persian poet, c1300

We Librans need beauty in our lives every bit as much as we need oxygen, and no good purpose is served by pretending that we can do without it. We can't, and that's the honest truth. But there are many subtle changes of approach we can use to help us reduce the amount of money we spend on surrounding ourselves with the visual delight that we crave.

Do you love paintings, art, sculpture and fine ceramics or fine jewellery? Make a point of paying regular visits to art galleries and museums to feed your appetite for beauty. Another approach is to learn to make paintings and pieces of pottery and sculpture yourself. Take it from me, there is little that is more satisfying than admiring an exhibition of one's own watercolours. Or treat yourself to a huge bunch of seasonal flowers from a market. Whatever feeds your soul, just allow yourself to enjoy it, within the limits of your spending plan.

"I now surround myself with
beauty every day."

Individuality

"Fashion fades. Only style remains."

Coco Chanel

We Librans love to look well dressed at all times, but look-ing good doesn't mean you have to be a slave to fashion. The only way to really derive value from your wardrobe is to get in touch with the kind of styles that work best for you, given your particular type of look.

Spend an afternoon playing "dress-up" in a large depart-ment store, and experiment with as many different styles as you can lay your hands on. Do you look better in long jackets or short? Is your best look crisply tailored or softly romantic? Long or short skirts, pants or culottes? When you have established your own particular "look", you can add the finishing touches that really help create your indi-vidual style. What does it for you? Is it your hairstyle, or the handmade earrings you love to wear? Your ethnic necklaces, or Indian silk scarves?

Once you have found your style, you will find that your buying "mistakes" magically dwindle away. Welcome to the brave new world of conscious clothes shopping!

"I now discover my own individual style."

Self-Development

"We are traditionally rather proud of ourselves for having slipped creative work in there between the domestic chores and obligations. I'm not sure we deserve such A-pluses for that."

Toni Morrison

One reason we Librans can sometimes overindulge in retail therapy is that we haven't taken the time and trouble to discover who we really are… Our lives may be going along smoothly, but all the while, niggling away at the back of our subconscious is the unlived life that is burning to express itself. Many Librans have fine creative and intellectual gifts, but we can so easily get caught up in making other people's lives work, that we don't make enough time for our own dreams and ambitions.

Is there something that you are really longing to do? Write a book? Take art classes? Learn French and go live in Paris for six months?

Today, take time to touch base with your secret longings and commit them to paper in your notebook. And promise yourself that you will do at least one thing every day towards making your own dreams come true.

"I now make my own self-development my first priority."

Financial Equilibrium

"If your outgoings exceed your income, then your upkeep will be your downfall."

Bill Earle

As Librans, our sign is symbolised by the scales – and with our taste for the good life, we know all too well how easy it is for our spending to tip the balance in the wrong direction. Or do we? Maybe, if we are truly honest with ourselves, our decorating skills also include the ability to do a great "wallpaper job" on our finances. Today, it's time to face up to facts and look at the reality of our true financial situation.

Are you spending more than you earn? If you don't know then you need to find out. Go back to the Counting exercise (see Gemini). If your outgo does exceed your income, then the exercise will show you where your financial weak spots are. Nobody says you have to give up anything forever – this is not like a diet, you are not being punished. It's just time to get real about money, and see where you may need to make some changes.

"I now embrace the reality of my financial situation."

Decisiveness

"Changes are calling to you. Can you hear them?
Doors that have been closed are opening wide.
Can you see them?
New pathways are appearing right before you eyes.
Will you follow them?
As it says in the Talmud: if not now, then when?

Barbara De Angelis

With Venus as our planetary ruler, we sometimes shrink from making decisions, as we are terrified that we will choose badly – and other people will get mad at us as a result. But the major choices we make in life really are life's milestones - and if we persist in avoiding decisions, then our lives will be as other people want them to be, not as we our-selves have fashioned them. And we will merely be living our lives by default. It doesn't sound very satisfying, does it?

We need to learn that decision-making is a necessary part of life, and that our choices, as well as our partner's, are valid too. Surely it's better to live the life that we have cho-sen, even if we make a few mistakes along the way, than to live a life that others have chosen for us?

If you have important decisions to make right now, take time to weigh all the factors you need to consider. Your choices do matter. As screenwriting guru Robert McKee points out, "Characters reveal themselves by the choices they make under pressure." What do your choices reveal about you?

"I now allow myself the time I need to make the right choices."

Boundaries

"Two major issues complicate our lives above all else. The first is our ongoing battle with consumerism … the second challenge is the tendency for many of us to say Yes, when we'd like to say No."

Elaine St James

As Librans, our lives are often rendered unbearably complicated by our impossibly idealistic attempts to please all the people all the time. The fact is, this is simply not possible – nor should we even try. "But if I do x, y, z (don't turn up for Christmas dinner, don't baby-sit my sister's kids, don't lend my boyfriend my new car) they won't like me, wails Libra. Well, so they don't like you? So what? Will the world really come to an end if they don't?

As the writer and metaphysician Stuart Wilde is so fond of pointing out, "What other people think of you is none of your business." The fact is, we often spend too much of everything – time, money, energy – trying to keep other people happy, when really we need to please ourselves a whole lot more.

Would your financial situation be better if you allowed yourself to say "No" occasionally? Food for thought isn't it? Saying "No" can often be the first step along the road to inner freedom. As an exercise, the next time someone asks you to do something you really don't want to do, just try saying "No". You may just rather like the way it feels…

"I now allow myself the freedom to say No, as well as Yes."

Creative Visualization

"The world of reality has its limits; the world of the imagination is boundless."

Jean-Jacques Rousseau

We Libran women are blessed with razor-sharp minds and fabulously vivid powers of imagination. So it's up to us to use these gifts in our journey toward making our dreams come true. One of the most potent tools that exist for improving our life situation is creative visualization. Through forming images of the results we wish to bring about in our lives, and focusing on these images regularly, we can help create major shifts and changes in our external lives.

I know from my own experience what an incredibly powerful tool creative visualization can be, for the first apartment I ever owned in London was one that I had been regularly visualizing for a year or so beforehand. Indeed, when I came to view the place, I didn't even need to go inside before deciding to buy it, because the outside looked identical to the apartment I had been visualizing!

One last point – we also need to be detached about the images we are visualizing – because if our goals don't truly serve our growth and Highest Good, they probably aren't going to happen...

"I now use the power of creative thought to create my own Highest Good."

♈ ♉ ♊ ♋ ♌ ♍ ♎ ♏ ♐ ♑ ♒ ♓

♏︎

Scorpio

"I know the bottom ... I know it with my great tap root. It is what you fear. I do not fear it. I have been there."

Sylvia Plath

Passion

"Desire is good. Passion is good. A passionate desire Focuses the will, which allows energy to move...when we have the courage to desire with passion and precision, the Universe responds..."

Julia Cameron

We Scorpios have a reputation throughout the known universe for our supposed skill in the arts of the bedroom – but truth be told, it's our passion for life that really distinguishes us from other mortals. Scorpios need to care – truly, deeply, madly – about whatever it is they are doing, otherwise they might as well not bother turning up to do it.

Scorpios need passion – and the Scorpio without a cause has a nasty habit of turning all that searing, soulful energy in on herself – hence our time-honoured reputation for self-destructive behaviour which naturally includes overspending.

Today, take time out to have a long, cool look at the kind of work and activities (relationships count too) you are involved in at the moment. Do your current projects and partnerships excite and inspire you, and fill you with passion? If not, you need to ask yourself why you're doing them ... then take your notebook, and write a list of goals that would fill you with passion. Start thinking about what you can do today to make those goals happen.

"I now connect with my true inner passion."

Grace

"If only we all knew that each of us always has two guardian angels with us. These angels are here to help and guide us, but we must ask for this help. They love us very much and await our invitation."

Louise Hay

Thanks to the wonderful resurgence of interest in angels in recent years, we're all much more familiar with the idea that we are surrounded by loving beings of spiritual grace – but they can only help us if we ask for their help. We can experience miracles every day if only we are open to them. That is if we remember to ask for a miracle to happen. For although we are surrounded by angelic beings, universal law dictates that they can only help us if we actively seek their guidance.

If you have established your quiet time or meditation period, try experimenting by adding a few "angel prayers" at the end. If you are desperate for money to pay your bills, just ask your angels. Every day, if need be! If you want a new job, or solutions to pressing relationship problems, just ask your angels. Write your prayers down on paper too.

Another lovely idea is to write a letter to your guardian angel and tuck it away in your bible. But do remember to ask, and keep on asking…

"I now ask my angels for their help and guidance every day."

Surrender

"We trade a life that we have tried to control and we receive in return something better – a life that is manageable."

Melody Beattie

Many Scorpio women know what it's like to have life become so problematic and difficult that you just don't feel you can go on anymore. Whether we're grappling with financial problems or some problem stemming from addiction, we can literally become exhausted from the sheer effort of trying to hold it all together.

The great news is, we really don't have to do this. We don't have to be control freaks, because there is always an answer, and God always knows what that answer is. All we have to do is turn it over to the universe, and wait for the answers to come. But I do mean really turn it over...

It has been my own personal experience that just when things looked blackest, if I just let go and allowed life to take its course, the answers would come. Miracles do happen. Horrendous financial difficulties can be resolved in this way – trust me. But you have to believe that miracles can happen, and you have to be willing to let them happen. Ask for the answers to your problems, and then be totally detached as to the outcome...

"I now surrender to the process of life."

Magnanimity

"Many speak the truth when they say that they despise riches, but they mean the riches possessed by other men."

Charles Caleb Cotton

Living in a state of financial serenity means that we feel happy and pleased when we see other people doing well. Does this sound like you? Be honest, now. Envy is a classic Scorpio flaw, and sadly, we can suffer from the green-eyed monster on a distressingly regular basis – like daily! But if we don't feel calm when we see our friends getting the great job, the great relationship, the great house, the unexpected windfall, etc, it's because the other person's success is triggering our own sense of lack. Put simply, we are afraid that our good isn't coming, that someone up there has forgotten to send down a parcel of goodies with our name on it…

"A Course in Miracles" teaches that there are only two states of being in life – love or fear. Fear blocks out all the good things in life and encourages a feeling of lack and separation. So when we give into our feelings of jealousy, we are simply showing how fearful we are. When we choose to feel abundant and financially serene instead, we can relax into living our lives, in a state of positive expectancy. As a wise man once said, "God's delays are not God's denials". We just have to be prepared to be a little bit more patient sometimes!

"I am a truly abundant being, and all my needs and wants are met."

Non-Attachment

*"Money, it turned out, was exactly like sex.
You thought of nothing else if you didn't have it,
and thought of other things if you did."*

James Baldwin

It's said that money can't buy you happiness (all it can do is allow you to be miserable in comfort) but it's truly amazing how many people believe that all their problems would be solved if they only had more money. As even the super-rich Scorpio Bill Gates has discovered however, having vast amounts of money just brings you a different class of problem!

Poverty is stressful, and I wouldn't dream of advocating it for moment. But in my experience, the truly wealthy people in this life are those who live within their means (however limited they happen to be) and then get on with the far more important business of doing whatever it is they came to the planet to do – be that writing, publishing, singing, making music, whatever...

Money just isn't an end in itself, only a means to an end, no matter how hard we think otherwise. We are wise not to forget that. Take time today to think of all the real things in your life that money couldn't buy you and write them down in your notebook.

**"I trust that money will manifest in my life, in
proportion to my needs and wants."**

Purification

"I have learned by some experience ... that certain environments, certain modes of life, certain modes of conduct are more conducive to inner and outer harmony than others ... simplification of life is one of them."

Anne Morrow Lindbergh

We Scorpio women have passionate natures that can lead us to behave in a generally excessive manner. We often do too much, spend too much, eat too much, drink too much, etc, etc. So we need to set aside certain times each year when we take a break from our hectic lifestyles and just simplify, simplify, simplify...

Ideally we need to take ourselves off to a cleaner, simpler environment. A log cabin close to a lake, or the seashore, would be ideal! We need to de-toxify our systems by eating a pure diet with lots of fruit, vegetables, grains and pulses, and placing limits on alcohol and caffeine. Fasting from the mass media also helps – avoid television, newspapers and telephones for a few days, if possible!

As the complications of your everyday life begin to fade into the background, you will begin to get a good sense of where you are on track with your life – and by implication, where you are not. Take your notebook, and jot down the intuitive promptings that enter your mind. What changes do you need to make? Following a purification regime for a few days each year will help you to find out.

"I now commit myself to purifying and simplifying my life."

Freedom

*"I prefer the luxury of freedom from a job to the
luxury of material goods."*
                                        Amy Dacyczyn

As Scorpios, we value personal freedom above almost anything else in life. Freedom, to a Scorpio is a state of being
more precious than rubies. We have an overwhelming dis-
like of being told what to do by others, and we love being our
own boss and running our own show. Sometimes, however,
we fail to understand the connection between our financial
behaviour and the level of personal freedom that exists in
our lives, for these two things are inextricably linked.

The plain fact is, the less money you spend on nonessential
items (and you alone know what these constitute for you),
the freer you will be. The lighter your financial commitments (the smaller your mortgage, rent payments, etc), the
freer you will be. The less personal debt you carry, the
freer you will be. I have seen people say that they want to
take a year off to write a novel, travel round the world, etc
– but all too often, their financial behaviour isn't support-
ing that goal, since they continue to fritter money away on
stuff they don't really value or enjoy.

Ask yourself today, what's more important to you?
Feeling free to do what you want with your life – or simply
going shopping?

*"I now acknowledge my need for
personal freedom."*

Constructive Action

"Constructive actions align us with abundance."

Natasha Hoffmann

We Scorpios are co-ruled by Mars, the planet of war – which means that when we don't feel life is going our way, we're capable of throwing the most spectacular tantrums and displays of temper on the planet. Truth be told, however, all that emotional energy we burn up in giving vent to our rage and dumping it on the nearest bystander, innocent or otherwise, could always be better used in other ways. Emotional thunderstorms don't do anybody any good, least of all ourselves.

How we spend our energy is how we spend our lives – so when you feel inclined to let rip with your temper, why not think about pouring that energy into clearing out your closet or weeding your garden instead? By the time your rage has abated, you'll have achieved something positive – and that, in turn, will make you feel better about yourself.

So, the next time someone upsets you, press the "pause" button on your emotional reactions, and ask yourself, "If I lose my temper here, will this help me achieve my goals?" If the answer is No, think about doing something that WILL help achieve those goals instead. In other words something constructive.

"I now aim to act constructively at all times."

Inheritance

"Saving is a very fine thing. Especially when your parents have done it for you."

Sir Winston Churchill

With Pluto as our planetary co-ruler, we Scorpios often have a great deal to do with wills, inheritances, and "the goods of the dead". When we are lucky enough to receive an inheritance, it's appropriate that we consider the best way to spend that money and treat it with due respect, for it may well represent the fruits of another person's lifetime of labour. Money is a form of universal energy and needs to be respected as such. If we don't know enough about investments to handle the money properly, it's important that we employ advisers of integrity.

If you receive an inheritance, no matter how small, it's important to express gratitude to the universe and to the dead, for the freedom that this money will give you. It's also appropriate that we spend some time considering the nature of our non-financial inheritance too. What are the spiritual qualities that we have inherited from our parents or grandparents? Do we have their strength of character, their staying power or perhaps their patience, their humour? We need to be grateful for both our financial and "invisible" inheritances too…

"I now give thanks for all the good
I have inherited."

Meticulousness

"What do we do when we are depressed, when we are lonely, when we feel unloved? More often than not, we buy something to make use feel better ... we have learned to seek external solutions to signals from the mind, heart or soul that something is out of balance."

Joe Dominguez and Vicki Robin

Deep down, we know when our lives are out of whack, although our mad spending binges and credit card excesses may seem innocent enough. After all, no one ever got locked up for shopping too much! Not unless they actually stole to finance their habit, that is...

But what we are really trying to do is, to spend the pain away, to compensate ourselves for the lack of something very significant in our lives, whatever that something is. It could be a lack of mothering or fathering in childhood, perhaps because our parents themselves were emotionally unavailable or suffered from addiction: it could be pain and sorrow at the burden of our unlived lives, and unanswered creative urges: it could be pain at the fact that we feel we never get a chance to really be ourselves.

Whatever our hidden issue is, it's up to us to take steps to deal with it, whether those steps involve our finding a therapist or enrolling in a 12-Step programme. You alone know how bad the problem is ... and you alone hold the key to finding a solution.

"I now take responsibility for my feelings and my finances."

Forgiveness

"To err is human - to forgive is not our policy."

Anonymous

When it comes to forgiving those poor mortals who have had the sheer impudence to offend us, we Scorpio women do a pretty good imitation of the Snow Queen. But long-standing grudges are a heavy burden to carry through life, and rob us of vital life energy – energy that we badly need in order to lead a more creative life.

Another dimension of our Scorpionic lack of forgiveness is that we are also extremely slow to forgive ourselves for our own transgressions. We feel we should get everything right first time, and beat ourselves up mercilessly when we don't. Aside from anything else, this is highly unrealistic. Think how children learn to walk – and consider the fact that we are all in the never-ending process of learning how to live.

Today, take your notebook and make a list of all the people in your life that you need to forgive – and a second list of all the things you would like to forgive yourself for. You can also add a "Forgiveness Minute" to your daily meditation if you want to.

**"I am now willing to forgive myself
and others."**

Giving

"Love lives by giving and forgiving, Self lives by getting and forgetting."

Sathya Sai Baba

Along with our opposing sign of Taurus, we Scorpios have a tendency to be distinctly possessive by nature. Just like toddlers with their toys, we have a clear sense of what's "mine" and we rarely hesitate to enforce it. But as we slowly evolve a more spiritual perspective on the whole business of money and possessions, we come to understand that our true relationship to the material plane is actually one of stewardship.

The universe gives us houses, cars, clothes, objects, etc for our use while we are here on the planet – but eventually we will have to let go of all the things we "own" when we die.

We Scorpios often find it hard to give and share, but if we experiment with tithing – the ancient law of increase – we can discover its timeless truth. Today, give away a percentage (you choose the exact figures) of time or money to an organization whose values you admire: this affirmation of your own abundance will soon draw its own reward.

"I am happy to share a part of all I have."

♈ ♉ ♊ ♋ ♌ ♍ ♎ ♏ ♐ ♑ ♒ ♓

Sagittarius

"It is better to live rich than to die rich."

Samuel Johnson

Celebration

"If I were the master of the universe, I would change all the rules for holiday gift-giving. In my tightwad utopia, I would decree the following: gifts shall not be given simply for the sake of giving a gift; gifts shall be given only according to each individual's resources and inspiration."

Amy Dacyczyn

Given our penchant for extravagance and high living, perhaps it's no coincidence that we Sagittarians are born in the most spendthrift season of the year – namely, the run-up to the great Christmas spendfest. This is Jupiter's season, those few mad weeks when we all flex the plastic to the limit and beyond, and usually live to regret it.

If the Christmas holidays generally leave you with a spending hangover, why not think about doing things a little differently this year? Firstly, plan well ahead. The best bargains are to be had all year round, so when you see a suitable gift, buy it and stash it away till next year. Buy your Christmas decorations straight after New Year when they are on sale. Think about making some presents this year. Can you sew, cook or paint? What could be nicer than a hand-painted picture, personalised herbal pillow or bottled preserves? Avoid throwing parties in restaurants, and entertain at home instead. Hire or borrow ball gowns – don't buy them. Offer to DO things as your gift to others – like a massage, or childminding, for instance.

Finally, do your spending sprees on paper – choose everything you want from mail order catalogues, fill in the forms, but don't post them! You'll feel like you've been shopping for real...

"I now rejoice in simple festivals and celebrations."

Appropriateness

"True financial independence is understanding that if you buy now, you WILL pay later – with interest. Financial independence is knowing that if you spend your life energy on stuff that brings only passing fulfilment and doesn't support your values, you end up with less life."

Joe Dominguez and Vicki Robin

For Sagittarians, part of the secret of attaining financial serenity is learning how to create a lavish lifestyle on a limited income. With Jupiter as our planetary ruler, we hate to feel "mean", but if we are to avoid living in debt our whole lives we need to make wise spending choices, according to our means. We need to learn how to set realistic budgets for the things we long to do. We need to learn how to plan properly, instead of buying on impulse and living on endless credit.

Every time you go to spend money, ask yourself, does this expenditure really support my values? Am I really getting value for money here? Is there a way I could have this experience without spending so much? For example if you want a large house, go for a "fixer-upper" with lots of space that you can refurbish at your leisure. Find friends who can help you, and trade services for their help. If you're downshifting and leaving the city for the countryside, maybe you have a friend or friends who could come and help you renovate, in exchange for room and board. As Sagittarians, it's not easy for us to do this, but evaluating the real cost of what we buy is an important lesson to learn.

"I now spend money appropriately, and in accordance with my true life values."

Precision

*"You cannot ask us to take sides against arith-
metic. You cannot ask us to take sides against
the obvious facts of the situation."*

Sir Winston Churchill

As Sagittarians, one of the most important life lessons we
need to learn is that of attention to detail. We love the big
picture, the large canvas of our lives, those bold, broad
brush-strokes, but we often get bored stiff dealing with the
details. We usually apply the same principle to our
finances, and this is how we can come badly unstuck.

The fact is, we may not be particularly interested in the
details of how much money we are really earning, but it is
important that we know. We may not really be interested
in how much money we are really spending, and on what,
but it is important that we know.

Like it or not, we need to learn to "do the arithmetic" of
our current life situation, and reflect on the implications of
our calculations. If you haven't followed the Gemini step,
"Counting" yet, buy a small cash book and write down
everything you spend for at least one month, as well as
what you earn. At the end of the month, divide your
spending into categories, so you can see where your
money is going. Just do it!

**"I now take time to calculate my true
financial position."**

Peace

"Just as negative addictions sneak up on us a day at a time, so do positive cravings. Meditation, creative movement, moments of self-nurturing that bring contentment – all can become positive habits of well-being."

Sarah Ban Breathnach

As Sagittarians, we are often quite restless by nature, leaping from one experience to another … but if we can take the time to connect with the reservoir of stillness that lies within us, the peace that we find there will have a positive impact on every other area of our lives, including our finances.

Make time every day for a short period of meditation – even fifteen minutes will make a difference. Clear your mind, and watch your breath. You may find that the voice of your intuition begins to speak to you during this quiet time. Pay attention to what is said. Given time, your restlessness will start to subside, and you will experience a newfound longing to connect with these peaceful feelings every day. Gentle, creative movement such as yoga or tai chi can also produce a similar effect.

"I now take time each day to enter the stillness within me."

Self-Discovery

"Money does not change people. It only unmasks them."

Mme Riccoboni

The "stuff" we Sagittarians choose to surround ourselves with speaks volumes about us – but does your current lifestyle truly reflect your inner nature? Sometimes we overspend to keep up a lifestyle we have outgrown, purely out of habit, or our desire to keep up appearances – when deep within, a new, creative, more streamlined version of ourselves is struggling to emerge.

Since images and pictures enable us to connect directly with the unconscious mind, they can be very valuable tools to self-discovery. A great technique is to take five or six magazines (interior design and homemaking glossies are good for this exercise) and cut out all the pictures that really strike you. Don't think too much while you're doing this – just tear out pictures quickly. Get a large piece of paper and stick on the pictures with paper glue, arranging them as you wish. What are the pictures saying to you? You can also use movie images to assist this process of self-discovery. Take your notebook, and write out a list of your five favourite films. Are there any common themes that stand out? Are these themes currently finding expression in your life?

These exercises can provide valuable clues as to what's working and what isn't working in your current lifestyle. You may feel inspired to make some major changes as a result – be warned!

"I now take time to connect with my authentic, inner self."

Walking

"If you are seeking creative ideas, go out walking. Angels whisper to a woman when she goes for a walk."

Raymond Inmon

We Sagittarians adore the great outdoors and being close to nature helps put us directly in touch with our powers of intuition. Taking a walk every day also gives us space to reflect on our plans and actions, and the way in which we are using our available resources of time, energy and money. Use this time out from your everyday life to mull over your spending, and ask yourself whether your expenditures accord with your personal values. You may also find that creative "flashes of inspiration" and business ideas come to you during this time.

Go out walking every day if you can, and listen to the ideas that bubble up in your mind. Put them into action when you return home.

"I now care for myself by talking a walk every day."

Temperance

"There are two sides to the coin of living beyond your means. The shiny side is that you can have everything you want right now. The tarnished side is that you will pay for it with your life."

Joe Dominguez and Vicki Robin

With Jupiter as our planetary ruler, we Sagittarians need to face the fact that we can often be just plain spendthrift. It must have been a Sagittarian who invented the phrase, "Live now, pay later", for we rarely lose sleep at night worrying whether we've charged too much on our credit card today…

But over and above simply living the good life, however, we Sagittarians also treasure our freedom. We want to be free to pursue our life's dreams – and not feel chained to a job. But we need to really understand that our spending habits can sabotage our dreams, by burdening us with debts that must be serviced.

When we feel that our debts are getting out of control, drastic action is sometimes called for. Trying paying for all your purchases in cash for a week, and see how it feels to be financially "sober". It probably won't feel that great to begin with, but it's a far surer route to financial serenity than an ever-expanding your credit card debt.

"I now allow myself to use credit wisely."

Self-Awareness

"She who knows others is wise; she who knows herself is enlightened."

Lao-Tzu

For us Sagittarian women, one vital aspect of achieving financial serenity is knowing our own strengths and weaknesses. Generally speaking, on the positive side, we are great visionaries and entrepreneurs, the champion risk-takers of the zodiac – but on the downside, we can sometimes be careless and impatient about taking care of our resources. To put it another way, we are often a lot better at making money than looking after it…

For the sake of our financial serenity, we need to be brutally honest with ourselves about this. Looking over our past financial performance may help! If there is any financial slack in our lives, we may need to find the right people to help deal with it. We need a good book-keeper (maybe) and a good accountant (definitely). Having a good lawyer is also essential, for dealing with contracts. Start assembling your team today!

"I am willing to be honest with myself about my financial strengths and weaknesses."

Completion

"Creating anything new and fresh works much better if you mindfully "complete" what is finished at the same time that you are dreaming up the new."

Christiane Northrup MD

As Sagittarians we are deeply mutable by nature, and we thrive on change, variety and freshness. We are always longing to gallop on ahead to the next project… We love nothing better than new ideas but in order to move on, we also need to reach closure with whatever projects we are currently engaged on. The fact is, we love to paint the picture, but we hate to wash the brushes. Oh, couldn't someone else do that, we murmur?

Sagittarians are sometimes guilty of a lack of thoroughness, and we need to learn to pay more attention to detail – especially where the financial details of our lives are concerned. We do need to learn to read our contracts thoroughly, and study the small print, even if we find it "boring". Failing to do this can have severe financial consequences.

Today, take an honest look at all the "unfinished business" in your life, and promise yourself you will achieve closure and completion where you can.

"I am now willing to complete the unfinished business in my life."

Vision

*"One can never consent to creep when one feels
an impulse to soar."*

Helen Keller

The wonderful thing about being a Sagittarian is that our
dreams are so much bigger than everyone else's! How is it
that so many filmmakers, the Steven Spielbergs of this
world, are born under this sign? Simple – because they
allow themselves the freedom to dream their dreams, and
to believe that other people will help make those dreams
come true.

With Pluto transiting through Sagittarius since the mid-
1990s, many Sagittarians feel they have had to tailor and
streamline their dreams quite radically. But the world of
the imagination would perish without vision, and we all
need Sagittarians to carry on dreaming those dreams.

Today, take time to connect with your own dreams for the
future. Who can help you make those dreams happen?
What steps can you take today, and during the days that
follow to make your dreams come true? What financial
resources will you need? Write it all down, because writing your dreams down is the first step to making them
come true…

*"I now connect with my greatest dreams
for the future."*

Risk Management

"I never attempt to make money on the stock market. I buy on the assumption that they could close the market the next day and not reopen it for five years."

Warren Buffett

As honorary children of Jupiter, the most optimistic God on Mount Olympus, we Sagittarians thrive on taking risks. But for the sake of our financial serenity, we need to be sure that the risks that we take are those ones where the odds are heavily weighted in our favour.

One mistake we often make is that of thinking that good things are going to last forever. How many Sagittarians were snared by volatile techno-stocks and "dotcom" companies, or over-inflated commercial property deals, for example?

Financial astrologer Daniel Pallant notes that Sagittarians are often irresistibly drawn to the futures market, and can often end up losing their shirt in the process. With a little more prudent speculation, such losses can be avoided. Today, remind yourself that all business are cyclical, and ask yourself honestly if you are being over-optimistic about your current investment strategy. Get a second opinion, if need be.

"I now balance optimism with prudence in all my investments."

Travelling

*"There's a helluva great universe next door.
Let's go."*

e e cummings

We Sagittarians were born with itchy feet, and there are few things we love more than travelling and taking vacations. Our restless nature and love of travel can often make a huge dent in our bank balance, however, so we need to learn to indulge our passions wisely.

The tragic events of September 11th 2001 have also made some of us far less willing to travel by air – so maybe we can make some "downshifting-type" changes to the way we travel and take vacations.

Instead of going to Europe next summer, why not think of taking a low-cost camping vacation instead? Spending leisure time closer to home can be just as satisfying and far less costly than overseas travel. Investigate other low-cost options too. If you're young and single, why not think of travelling as a courier? Opt for house-swaps instead of hiring holiday cottages and villas. Also keep an eye out for the many great last-minute travel bargains you can find on the internet.

"I now travel according to my means."

♈ ♉ ♊ ♋ ♌ ♍ ♎ ♏ ♐ ♑ ♒ ♓

♑

Capricorn

"I conceived it as my task to create difficulties everywhere."

Søren Kierkegaarde

Positive Thinking

*"Bless a thing and it will bless you. Curse it
and it will curse you. If you bless a situation, it
has no power to hurt you, and even if it is troublesome for a while, it will gradually fade out if
you sincerely bless it."*

Emmet Fox

With Saturn as our planetary ruler, we Capricorns are
steeped in earthly virtues. We are reliable, hardworking
and conscientious to a fault – but our Achilles heel often
lies in our penchant for negative thinking. Left to our own
devices, we invariably expect the worst. Since our
thoughts will eventually tend to mirror our reality, we
often receive what we expect. But think – would you
rather live out your nightmares or your dreams?

The antidote to this vicious circle of negativity lies in positive thinking – in consciously cultivating the habit of
expecting good things, in our day-to-day life, in our relationships and our finances.

If you are currently stuck in a difficult situation, use it as a
testing ground to try out the power of positive thinking.
Just as an exercise, for one week aim to stop all negative
thoughts in their tracks as soon as they appear, and replace
them with positive ones. Negative thinking is a habit, but
it's an unhelpful habit – and positive thinking can become
a habit too – if you persevere with it.

**"I now allow myself to think positively
at all times."**

Joyfulness

"Do what you love, the money will follow."

Marsha Sinetar

We Capricorns pride ourselves on our efficient and dutiful nature, but how many times do we allow ourselves the unalloyed pleasure of doing what we most enjoy?

We begin by denying ourselves the smaller pleasures of life: we don't allow ourselves to buy the food we want, or the clothes we want, "because they're too expensive" – and then the habit spreads to the bigger issues in our life – such as our work. We don't allow ourselves to do the work we love because we're afraid it isn't "practical" – we're afraid we won't have enough money to pay our bills and meet our financial commitments, etc.

Truth be told, the only reliable route to a life of abundance and financial serenity lies in doing what we love for a living, rather than what we "ought" to do. Today resolve to eliminate the "oughts" and "shoulds" from your life, as much as possible. Take baby steps. Allow yourself to do the things you enjoy for half an hour a day, to begin with. Get clear about what it is you love to do most. And allow yourself to entertain the possibility that you could really do it for a living…

"I now allow myself to do what I love."

Success

"The need to win – now! – is a need to win approval from others. As an antidote, we must learn to approve of ourselves. Showing up for the work is the win that matters."

Julia Cameron

We Capricorns can be exceedingly goat like in our nature, and there's nowhere we like being more than right there on top of the mountain. The downside of this is that if we don't scale those dizzy summits fast enough for our liking, we often become racked with self-loathing and fall head-long into depression. That's when our spending can some-times go awry, as we attempt to console ourselves for our imaginary lack of achievement.

The truth is, such Capricorn competitiveness is really just the ego talking – since "success" is a totally subjective judgement. For example, some writers don't think they're successful until they make it on to the New York Times best-seller list – other writers think they're doing really well when they manage to finish a short story!

Today, think about what constitutes "success" for you – and ask yourself whether your expectations are truly real-istic. Then, make a list of 20 things you are pleased with yourself for achieving in your life. Keep this list handy. Look at it whenever you feel like you haven't achieved enough in your life.

"I am a successful person in my own eyes."

Be Here Now

"Chase your passion, not your pension."

E J Olmos

We Capricorns truly are the master architects and virtuoso planners of the zodiac. We live to plan – but how do we plan to live?

When it comes to our finances, some of us plan them out as though we're going to live forever! Whilst it's wise and prudent to make adequate provision for our old age, it's also equally important that we allow ourselves sufficient money to enjoy life in the present moment. Don't get so caught up in planning your retirement fund that you deprive yourself of the financial resources you need to do what you want right now.

Remember - having all the money you could possibly wish for in your bank account is no safeguard at all against the hand of fate, when it deals an unforeseen blow – such as the death of a loved one, or the onset of a life-threatening disease…

Today, take your notebook and plan out how you can budget for vacations in the here and now (however modest they may be) as well as that cruise of a lifetime when you're sixty-five…

"I now allow myself to enjoy life in the present moment."

Balance

"Workaholism is a block, not a building block."
Julia Cameron

We Capricorns aren't often accused of being dizzy spenders, although we generally shop to impress, and can sometimes go totally over the top on buying designer labels. Our propensity for addictive behaviour tends to lie in less obvious areas, and we often get entangled in the invisible snares of workaholism.

We set unrealistic work targets for ourselves, and allow others to impose their equally unrealistic agendas on us. We regularly cancel outings with friends and family, and then wonder why we have no social life. We refuse to even contemplate taking a holiday that doesn't have a business element built in … no wonder we're exhausted – it's so hard to keep up with ourselves!

Today, if you feel that work has taken over your evenings and weekends, see how you can ransom back some time to spend just "being a human being." Start by banning work at weekends. Your social life should improve, as others find you more fun to be with!

"I now allow myself to work and play
in equal measure."

Empathy

"Co-operation is better than conflict."

Anonymous

With Saturn, the great cosmic teacher as our ruling planet, we Capricorns are always convinced that we know best. Very often, we end up holding the family purse strings – because it's what we're good at – and controlling them with a vicelike grip. It's usually we who make the major financial decisions in the family – but how often do we stop to take the opinions of other family members into account?

Ask yourself honestly, are you guilty of imposing your financial priorities on others? Did you insist that the family should all move to that big new executive home in that fashionable suburb, and forego summer holidays in order to cover the whacking great mortgage?

If this scenario strikes a chord with you, do resolve to try and involve others in the family's major financial decisions. Alienate others, and your own prosperity will be diminished. Aim for empathy instead and you'll find that others will also help you achieve your goals.

"I now consider the views of others when making major financial decisions."

Philanthropy

"A fund-raiser tried to persuade Hollywood movie producer Louis B. Mayer to give money to a charity "You know you can't take it with you." "If I can't take it with me", replied Mayer, "I won't go!"

Anonymous

This little story makes us laugh – but is that laughter perhaps a tad hollow because really, deep down, we do wish we could take it with us, and hang on to our hard-earned money forever?

In the eternal order of things, we are powerless to stop the ebb and flow of money in our lives, and we become wiser women when we acknowledge that salutary fact. It's a universal law that we need to circulate our money, not hang on to it for grim death. In addition, the more we let our money move around freely, the more money flows back to us in due course.

Even when we have money, we can sometimes become totally obsessed with the quest for the Holy Grail of bargain-hunting... Do you drive miles out of your way to save a few pennies on a can of paint? If so, money is still ruling your life, even though you may have plenty of it.

Today, resolve to loosen your grip a little. Give some money to your favourite charity or to a friend in need. Make it a gift, not a loan. And wait for the universe to send you an unexpected boon. Sooner or later, it will...

"I am now willing to share my good with others."

Detachment

"There are two main causes of ill-health in Western civilization. One of lack of job satisfaction – the other is over-rigid attachment to fixed outcomes."

Deepak Chopra

Another bittersweet fruit of our Capricorn obsession with goals and achievement is the pain we suffer when those goals don't come in on schedule. Don't get me wrong, it's good to have plans – and if we don't have goals in mind, we are like a ship setting off to sea without a rudder. But the secret of goal setting is, we need to be detached about the outcome of our efforts.

We need to act from the still centre of our being, and do the things we need to do, to make the creative contribution that we alone can make. We do need to have our dreams, and do all we humanly can to make them happen. And then we need to be totally relaxed about the outcome…

The ego hates this, of course, because uncertainty about the future drives it totally crazy. But we have to learn to live our dreams because that's what we love doing most – not because of where we think our dreams are going to take us. This process helps us to learn to love ourselves unconditionally, regardless of our achievements and this is a vital lesson for Capricorns to learn.

"I now allow myself to enjoy feeling detached about my goals."

Humility

"Just pretending to be rich keeps some people poor."

Anonymous

If we were granted an eagle's eye view of our lives, our superior vantage point would soon allow us to grasp the eternal truth that in the bigger picture of things, none of us really own anything – so our constant struggling to acquire more and more stuff will actually mean very little to us in the long run.

In the short term context of our day-to-day lives, however, it's easy to forget "the big picture". We Capricorn goats love to climb as high as we possibly can. And because we work so hard we usually manage to climb pretty high – but we sometimes fall into the trap of looking down on those who haven't managed to scramble as high up the mountain as we have. How much precious life do we waste amassing money to buy the right designer clothes and furniture, send our children to the right schools, pay for the country club sub-scription and make the payments on that massive mortgage?

Take a long, cool look at your spending habits, using the Counting step in Gemini. How much of your spending is done with the express goal of impressing others? If this sounds like you, try not to disparage the Have-Nots, and concentrate a little more energy on people, rather than things. Others will love you more for it in the long run and your life will be greatly enriched as a consequence...

"I now recognise and acknowledge my Oneness with all humankind."

Mentoring

"Share your knowledge. It's a way to achieve immortality".

The Dalai Luma

We Capricorns have a great deal of wisdom and knowledge that we could share with others, but we usually feel we are just too busy to stop and do so. But look back to the days when you yourself were starting out in your chosen career, and were so desperate to learn from others more experienced than yourself.

Were there people in your life who took the time to stop and give you a helping hand? Did you have a mentor, a wise older person whom you could turn to for advice? Remember, we are all part of the great Circle of Life – and the Circle of Life requires that you return the favours that have been bestowed upon you, and help others who are starting out on their own life journey.

For some Capricorns, giving time is harder even than giving money – but the important thing is to give. You choose the time and place. But make a point of giving…

"I now share my knowledge and experience with others."

Comfort

"Luxury need not have a price. Comfort itself is a luxury."

Geoffrey Beene

When we are born under the sign of Capricorn, being nice to ourselves doesn't always come as second nature. But until we learn to love and value ourselves, we are unlikely to achieve any degree of inner peace and serenity – financial or otherwise. Our relationships with others are also likely to fall somewhat short of the mark...

If you have spent a major part of your life trying to live up to other people's expectations, then learning to love yourself needs to be a top priority for you. Start small. Make your favourite foods for breakfast, or take yourself out for a cappuccino and croissant at your favourite café. Get rid of the outfits that make you feel stifled, constrained and dull (you know the outfits), and buy yourself something that makes you look and feel great. Start to make yourself more comfortable in every area of your life. Give yourself little treats, like your favourite magazines, or a small bottle of your favourite perfume. Designer labels don't necessarily make you feel more comfortable. Taking care of yourself does...

"I now allow myself to live my life in greater comfort."

Green Medicine

"Gardening is an instrument of grace."

May Sarton

As Capricorns, we often tend to live our lives too closely under the thrall of Saturn, and overlook the fact that Pan, the great god of nature, is also one of our ruling deities. Attuning ourselves to Pan helps us to loosen up a little and enjoy life more, and there is no better place to do this than in the garden!

If gardening isn't one of your hobbies at present, resolve to make it part of your lifestyle from now on, since few pursuits are more beneficial or therapeutic. Time spent in the garden breaks the thread of our workaholic striving and ambition, and reconnects us to the slower, more authentic cycles of nature.

A good way to find inspiration for starting your own garden – even if it's just a few pots of seeds on your kitchen windowsill – is to visit those gardens that have been crafted by other gardeners. My dear friend and fellow astrologer Helena Francis has created an astrological garden deep in the Surrey countryside. Your local tourist office is sure to have a list of "open gardens" you can visit. Gardening is blissfully habit-forming – the most important thing is simply to begin…

"I now open myself to the healing energies of nature."

♈ ♉ ♊ ♋ ♌ ♍ ♎ ♏ ♐ ♑ ♒ ♓

.

♒

Aquarius

"True equality can only mean the right to be uniquely creative."

Milton Erickson

Respect

"It's important to me that money not be important to me."

Les Brown

Being born under the sign of fixed air, we Aquarians are usually preoccupied with far more important matters than mere money – or so we like to think! We would happily endorse the thoughts of Henry Ford, who said, "Money is just what we use to keep tally...."

The fact is we Aquarians often don't take money that seriously at all. In fact, some of us take it so un-seriously that we can't even be bothered to log our spending, or pay our bills on time. Then we wonder why the telephone has been disconnected, and why quite a few unfriendly folks out there are trying to take us to court for our debts!

The bottom line is, we all have to deal with money. And the sooner we get used to the idea, the better. If we don't feel willing or able to look after our finances, we need to employ trustworthy professionals to help us with this vital aspect of our daily lives. But it simply isn't possible to just ignore money and hope that it will go away. It won't – and the more we try to ignore it, the worse our financial situation will become...

**"I now respect money as a form
of universal energy."**

Financial Simplicity

"One of the easiest ways I know to simplify your finances is to keep track of your monthly income and expenses so you can establish a workable spending plan to live within."

Elaine St James

Having faced the fact that we Aquarians often have little time or inclination to steward our finances, it's helpful to look at ways of making the whole process easier and more manageable for ourselves. Simplicity is the keyword here, and keeping it simple can help smooth our road to feeling more at ease around money.

In her book "Simplicity", Elaine St James, one of the leading American advocates of simple living, describes how she and her husband reduced the complexity of their financial chores by closing all but one bank account. They also eliminated all but a couple of credit cards, avoided consumer debt and consolidated their investment portfolio to within just a couple of families of funds. Their approach is a useful model for financial simplicity. Next, putting regular monthly payments on to direct debit can help you too, as long as the payment dates coincide with bank deposits.

The final step of this financial simplification process is to take your remaining "spending money" allocation out of the bank in cash – and write down what you spend it on. Try adopting this plan for one month, and see if how much easier it becomes for you to manage your finances.

"I now simplify the financial structures of my life."

Humanism

"The threads by which technology weaves the energies and materials of nature into our life are just as easily to be seen as fetters that tie us down, and make many things indispensable which even ought to be dispensed with, as far as the essence of life is concerned."

Georg Simmel

With the frugal planet Saturn as our ruler, we Aquarians often live quite modestly, and so we wonder how it is that we manage to run up considerable debts nevertheless. But our financial Achilles heel often lies in the fatal Aquarian weakness for new technology. Aquarius is the sign that's most closely linked with technical innovation, and many of us have a passion for trying out the latest and newest of anything and everything. Recognising that the problem exists is the first step to tackling our addiction.

You may need to take time to consider the impact of new technology on your life and the amount of time and energy you devote to it. Do you relate to machines better than people? Has surfing the net become a substitute for real human interaction? The answers to these questions may indeed make you resolve to lessen your reliance on technology ... which could also be good news for your finances.

"I am willing to consider the impact of technology on my life and my finances."

Interconnectedness

"What is good for an individual household is also good for the planet if it's done with vision and purpose."

Joe Dominguez and Vicki Robin

As Aquarians, we're usually way ahead of the crowd when it comes to considering new ways to conserve the environment and lessen the damage that is done to the planet through excessive consumerism. We like to think that all our actions are helping the greater community, as well as ourselves and our immediate family. So, when we're tempted to blow our budget on the latest gizmo that's captured our fancy, it helps if we can remind ourselves of the Green Triangle Effect.

The Green Triangle Effect works like this: whatever we can do to save personal resources and money usually has a positive effect on both our health and also the environment too. For example, if we choose to avoid using our car for short local journeys, and make these by foot or bicycle instead, we will save money, fuel and damage to the ozone layer. We will also benefit ourselves by taking exercise and getting fitter. Thus we save in 3 ways on eco-damage, fuel costs and gym subscriptions all in one go! Composting our vegetable waste cuts down on refuse bills and our purchase of artificial fertiliser, as well as reducing garbage collection and landfill. Trading clothes with a friend not only saves us money, but also benefits the environment by lessening the demand for manufactured goods. And so on…

"I now consider the effects of my spending habits on the environment."

Obedience

"Learn the rules so you know how to break them properly."

The Dalai Lama

With Uranus, the planet of revolution as our co-ruler, we Aquarians often grow up to be natural born rebels. But when it comes to our finances, this behaviour can be distinctly counterproductive. All too often, we spend a major part of our adult lives still caught in the teenage trap of financial rebellion against our parents.

We don't want to deal with paying our taxes, getting a mortgage, getting a "proper job" and balancing our cheque book because all that dumb stuff was just what our parents did, and we certainly don't want to be anything like them, no way! By choosing to perpetuate the childhood dance of anger with your parents, however, you are staying locked in old patterns, and are rendering yourself powerless to move forward in your life.

Ask yourself today, are you blocking your prosperity by staying trapped in habits of self-defeating rebellion? Wouldn't it be better to make your peace with the past and move on? If playing by the rules means dealing with money and paying our taxes, then the sooner we accept it, the sooner we will find financial serenity.

"I now accept the need to deal with money in an adult way."

Innovation

"Taking a new step, uttering a new word, is what people fear most."

Fyodor Dostoyevski

As children, we Aquarians often felt distinctly out of step with our peers, as though we were marching to the beat of a different drum – as indeed, we were! To be born under the sign of Aquarius generally means that we are always at least one step ahead of everyone else in our thinking, and in our lifestyle.

Rather than feeling bad about our futuristic thinking however, we need to learn to capitalise on it. Indeed, our talent for sensing future trends can often be the source of our financial fortune in life. We Aquarians are inventors and innovators, and our brain-children are often endowed with a streak of pure genius!

Today, promise yourself that you will start to share your inner wealth of new ideas with the world. Try to find a way of getting your ideas out there, even if it seems really hard to do this. The world needs your ideas, in order to move forward. Go to it!

"I now cherish and honour my talent for innovation."

Uniqueness

"If there is to be any peace, it will come through being, not having."

Henry Miller

As Aquarians, we often feel like we have little in common with the rest of the human race, because we tend to see the world a little differently from the way everyone else seems to … but we don't need to feel bad about this. Instead, we need to learn to say, "Vive la difference" and celebrate it!

We need to connect with a sense of our own uniqueness – so that instead of focussing on our innate differences in a negative way, we can learn to make the most of them.

Today, take time to consider what it is that makes you different from others, and where you feel your true gifts and talents lie. Maybe you haven't allowed yourself to start doing this up until now – but it is never too late to begin. Do you long to launch a business based on your ability to totally rethink an existing business sector? Do you long to work with children who are suffering because others see them as "different" in some way? Perhaps your ideas involve new approaches to conservation or the environment? Remember, you must first be who you are, before you can start living the life you want. Make a start today!

"I now embrace my own individuality and uniqueness."

Interdependence

"Call it a clan, call it a network, call it a tribe, call it a family. Whatever you call it, whoever you are, you need one."

Jane Howard

Although Saturn's powerful influence in our birth horoscope can often lead us to choose a solitary lifestyle, we Aquarians will never find happiness unless we include a few "significant others" in our game plan. Although we love nothing more than feeling independent, our obsession with self-sufficiency can sometimes cause us to feel lonelier than need be.

Ask yourself, don't you feel happier when you spend time with like-minded people – preferably a whole roomful of them?

Aquarius is the astrological sign of "the group", and we can enhance our prosperity by increasing our networking activities. If you work freelance, why not start a support group for like-minded professionals where you can exchange ideas and contacts? Hold a pot luck supper at least once a month, where friends can share both food and ideas. Join a LETS group (Local Exchange Trading Scheme) for bartering surplus goods and services in your area – if your town doesn't have one, why not think about starting one? Or start a wholefood and bulk-buying co-operative among your friends to save money and inspire a greater sense of community feeling ... and so on ...

"I now allow myself to enjoy feeling part of a group."

Timeliness

"Know the true value of time; snatch, seize and enjoy every moment of it. No idleness, no laziness, no procrastination; never put off till tomorrow what you can do today."

Lord Chesterfield

We Aquarians are often so preoccupied with dreaming up ideas for the future, that we forget to live in the "now". We often find it hard to manage our time as well as our money. Or maybe we make the mistake of thinking that we need huge stretches of uninterrupted time to get our ideas off the ground...

But since now, today, the present moment, is actually all we've got, we rob ourselves of prosperity and fulfilment if we don't make the most of each moment. If you have a project that you've been longing to make a start on, just take twenty minutes today to move it forward in some way. Write a letter, do some research, start drafting the introduction to that article or paper you want to write.

Another way of jump-starting ourselves into action is to travel forward in our imagination to our own funeral. Management guru Stephen Covey created this technique, and it's brilliantly effective. What is it you wish to be remembered for? Are you doing it yet? If not, hadn't you better get started?

"I now allow myself to make the most of every moment."

Ethics

"It is not how much one makes, but to what purpose one spends."

John Ruskin

Today, we need to ask ourselves whether the way we spend our money, has a positive or negative impact on the environment. The Quakers have a saying: "Where my money goes, there go I" – which is to say, "When I invest my money, it acts in the world as though I myself were there in person."

These days, we all need to take responsibility for investing consciously and wisely, and it's up to us to do the legwork to find out where our funds are being deployed. If we simply invest our money mindlessly, in a faceless institution, we may find that we are unwittingly helping to destroy the environment or worsen chemical pollution by backing companies that have a bad environmental track-record. These days, there are many excellent ethical funds available, so it's easier than ever to make sure that our money has a positive impact on the planet.

"I now spend and invest my money consciously and wisely."

Groundedness

*"She was so broke she couldn't even pay atten-
tion."*

American saying

Sometimes we find it so difficult to deal with things we
find "boring", such as keeping track of our money. We'd
far rather be dreaming up new ways to change the planet!
But we do need to remember that achieving financial equilibrium is a necessary foundation to doing the work we
really want to do. For if we are constantly fending off cred-
itors and landlords and dodging debt collectors, how can
we really give our life's work our full attention?

Taking responsibility for our spending, and making a commitment to healing our finances truly is an essential part of
healing our whole inner being. Dealing with money may
seem like a waste of time to us on one level, but if we don't
deal with financial issues as they arise, we will spend a dis-
proportionate amount of time dealing with them later,
when we may be fending off bankruptcy proceedings!

If you know in your heart that you aren't dealing with
your money matters in a grounded manner, make an
agreement here and now with yourself that you will
resolve to start doing so!

***"I now commit myself to handling my
money mindfully."***

Clustering

"Surround yourself with people who respect you and treat you well."

Claudia Black

With Saturn's influence strong in our Aquarian nature, many of us were raised in families where we were surrounded by relatives who were less than sympathetic to our dreams, goals and ambitions. We Aquarians may frequently have been told that we were "weird" or called "space cadets" – or words to that effect.

Choosing to pursue a path of financial serenity, however, means that we need to remind ourselves that we have the right to feel supported by people who will help us nurture our dreams, and encourage us to do what we love, knowing that the money will follow – eventually. Author and creativity guru Julia Cameron exhorts us to form "creative clusters" and seek out like-minded people who will support our ideas and our growth.

Today, take time to consider whether your friends and partners do truly support you. What kinds of things do they say? Do they come up with positive suggestions to help you further your ideas? Or are your "friends" dismissive and unsupportive? If so, you may need to consider ringing the changes in your circle of peers.

"I now surround myself with people who treat me with care and respect."

♈ ♉ ♊ ♋ ♌ ♍ ♎ ♏ ♐ ♑ ♒ ♓

♓

Pisces

"I am not confused. I'm just well mixed."

Robert Frost

Synchronicity

"Those unique coincidences which we call syn-chronistic make us aware, again and again, of the beauty, order and connectedness of the tales we are living."

Robert H. Hopcke

Have you ever noticed that once you make a definite decision to do something, people and events can often just fall into place in a meaningful way? You may be looking for a new place to live, and then a friend of a friend hears about a house that could be perfect for you. You turn up to view it, and the house number happens to be your "lucky number" … you walk inside, and the living room just happens to be painted in your favourite shade of blue. And so on!

A wise man once said that coincidences are God's way of helping us, whilst still remaining invisible. Unravelling the thread of synchronicity (Jung defined this as "meaningful coincidences") can launch you on the path to a truly magical way of living. If you go with the flow of coincidence, more and more grace will flood into your life and bless your journey. But if you say "No" to the help that is offered, life can soon become stagnant and dull.

Today, become alive to the thread of coincidence that is operating in your life… In myriad ways, your finances will, in all likelihood, improve, provided you keep following the thread.

"I am now open to having synchronicity work in my life."

Clarity

"God is love, but get it in writing."

Anita Loos

We Pisceans are among the most well-meaning people on the planet, but we sometimes suffer from a tendency to leave ourselves too many loose ends to trip up on. Just because we wouldn't dream of taking advantage of others, financially speaking, it seldom occurs to us that others might not be quite so honourable…

So in order to avoid misunderstandings, it's important to have clear agreements in all our financial and business dealings with others. Otherwise we may lose out financially.

In order to minimise the risk of woolly-headedness, try to keep your business and social life strictly separate. Doing business over lunch or dinner might work well for some, but it isn't always the ideal arrangement for you. If you have to do deals over dinner, avoid alcohol completely. Get people to put in writing what they expect of you, and vice versa, along with the precise terms of your remuneration. Be as clear as you possibly can, and then you won't end up disappointed and out of pocket.

"I am now totally clear in all my business and financial dealings."

Clear Boundaries

"Saying No can be the ultimate self-care."
Claudia Black

With Neptune as our planetary ruler, one of the hardest words for a Piscean to say is "No." In my opinion, all Pisceans should be made to practise saying this word at least 20 times in front of the mirror before they leave the house in the morning! This inability to say "No" stems from a deep-seated reluctance to upset other people ("I didn't want to hurt his feelings"), and it can lead many a sweet-natured Piscean into all sorts of difficulties.

The fact is, we Pisceans can often be the "soft touch" of the zodiac, and we often get drawn into lending people money we don't have, because we feel sorry for them. But if you are struggling to get your own act together, you're not really in a position to help others – and you need to face that fact.

When you feel you are in a position to help both you and others need to be clear about when any money lent is to be repaid – and how. Once again, it's a good idea to get it in writing, so there won't be any room for misunderstandings later. Also, there's the fact that you may be helping people to grow by not helping them out with a loan. As Sanaya Roman says, "it is important to know when to assist people and when not to."

"I now help others, within the limits of my ability to help."

Creative Expression

"The talents you possess are God's gift to you:
What you make of those talents is your gift to
God."

Anonymous

With Neptune, the planet of inspiration, as our planetary ruler, we Pisceans are among the most creatively gifted people on the planet. All too often, however, our inability to manage our finances in general, and our spending in particular, can sabotage our best efforts to express our creative gifts.

Learning how to handle money through the steps described in the foregoing meditations of Counting (see Gemini) and Financial Simplicity (see Aquarius) may be the necessary first steps on our creative career.

What do you feel is the channel for creative energy in your life? Many Pisceans are blessed with an innate gift for painting, music, singing and dance. If you have gifts, you need to start developing them now, regardless of how little time or money you possess at present. You may also discover that as you commit yourself to developing your potential, your finances will magically begin to become less of a problem in your life... There's never a right time to start – so why not start right now?

"I now accept the challenge of developing my
creative gifts."

Containment

"Mediaeval cities flourished within high walls that guarded their perimeters. Each of us contains a creative core that must be protected in precisely the same way. I think of my creativity as my most valuable asset. It is my wealth. I know that, and I protect it in the same way a wise man invests soundly and conservatively to protect his wealth."

Julia Cameron

When we start to develop our creative gifts and launch ourselves on the path to financial serenity through wiser management of our resources, we may often arouse the antagonism of those who have chosen a less inspiring path. It's important that we be aware of how sensitive we are, and how we need to protect ourselves, so that we don't get discouraged by the negative comments of others.

One way to do this is to only discuss your work and financial dreams with people that you know will be supportive. Surprisingly, this may not necessarily include your partner, spouse or family!

Today, make a list of those people who you know are really rooting for you to succeed. Make a point of discussing your dreams and projects, financial and otherwise, with those people only. There's no rule in the universe that says you have to tell your family everything. Especially if they're likely to be less than encouraging. Who needs "wet blankets"? You certainly don't…

"I now allow myself to protect my dreams."

Financial Routine

"It's not the tragedies that kill us, it's the messes."

Dorothy Parker

Each sign of the zodiac has many lessons to learn from its astrological opposite, which in Pisces' case just happens to be methodical, organised Virgo. So what can we take from the example of Ms Virgo aka She-Who-Is-Rarely-Overdrawn-At-The-Bank? The ability to get organised, mostly, and to create a routine, and stick to it...

This prospect most likely makes your eyes glaze over – it sounds kind of boring, right? But the truth is, becoming organized with a financial routine that works for us will actually free us up for our creative endeavours, not the reverse – in spite of all our fears.

The best way to create a financial routine and to keep on top of all your paperwork is to choose one day each month on which to do this. Preferably the first or last day of the month, so that it's an easy date to remember. Update your records on this day – file receipts and expenses, pay bills and analyse your spending log. That way, there won't be any unpleasant surprises when your taxes fall due.

Bribery works well, so promise yourself a reward for doing this, like a cappuccino or glass of mulled wine down at your favourite café. Choose the right time of day to do this too. If you're more alert in the evening, tackle your paper-work after dinner. If you're one of Nature's "larks", get the job over and done with first thing in the morning.

"I now establish a financial routine that works for me."

Inner Stillness

"The quieter we become, the more we can hear."

Ram Dass

We Pisceans always know what's "right" for us, if we will only allow ourselves the time and space to discover it. Truth be told, we are among the most intuitive signs of the zodiac, but we need the right conditions in order to develop our trust in our intuition. Every Piscean needs "down time," time alone when they are free to really "tune in" and listen to their inner voice...

If you don't have a quiet time as part of your daily routine already, then you need to establish one. Fifteen to twenty minutes each day can be enough to begin with. You may find that you enjoy it so much, you instinctively want to do more. You may find a gentle sense of "knowing" building within you, so that making major decisions is no longer so troublesome for you. Establishing a "quiet" time can also have positive effects on our spending patterns too, as we can allow ourselves the space to consider major purchases at leisure, and are no longer so prone to impulse spending, or making unwise financial decisions...

"I allow myself the space to tune in to my intuition."

Miracles

"I don't believe in miracles, I depend on them."

Paul Solomon

Miracles aren't just things that happened long ago in the Bible; they can happen to any of us, at any time, in our day-to-day lives. We Pisceans love to think about miracles too, as we have a great love of things that feel magical and can't be easily explained!

A miracle can be receiving just what you need at the time you most need it – like a loan that someone forgot to repay until now, or an unexpected break in your career when you have been plodding along patiently for a really long time…

Miracles can also take place when we allow ourselves to get free of addictive behaviours, such as overspending, gambling, or substance abuse, that have kept us captive for the longest time. If you want to cleanse your life of old habits and patterns and get the necessary help you need, ask for a miracle too. The simple fact is they seem to happen most often when we truly expect them to!

"I now expect a miracle."

Imagination

"You can bring things into your life rapidly by imagining you already have them".

Sanaya Roman

We Pisceans love to play make-believe and our penchant for acting "as if" something were true can be tremendously helpful on our journey to financial serenity. Dr. Wayne W Dyer writes that if you wish to be wealthy, it helps to start behaving generously, as though you have money to spare, by giving some away. Aim to do this without going into debt, of course – just give freely of whatever you have to spare, whether that happens to be time or money.

"Affirmative purchases" can also be a wise way of spending money, if they are carried out within reason. What are "affirmative purchases" you may ask? Well, by buying or making a delightful new set of cushions for the new home we long to buy, we are demonstrating to the universe our faith that we know it will deliver. By allowing ourselves little treats of the luxury items we love, we are showing the universe that we believe in the possibility of an expanded income and lifestyle.

Today, have fun thinking of ways you can play "make believe" in your life as it is right now, and thus create a new pathway for a life of greater prosperity. Take your notebook and make a "wish list" of the things you would like to have happen. Sign and date your list. When you look back over it in six months time, you may be amazed at how many of your wishes have in fact come true...

"I now allow myself to imagine a more prosperous way of life."

Perseverance

"We can do anything if we stick to it long enough."

Helen Keller

We Pisceans are dwellers of the ever-shifting ocean tides, and there's little we relish more than change and spontaneity in our lifestyle. But just as all the habits we have acquired take time to change, so too do we need to allow time to let our creative plans and projects take shape.

You cannot become a dancer, or an actor or a writer overnight, nor can you learn to make music in a matter of hours either. We Pisceans need to learn to resist the urges to give up and throw in the towel that can so easily threaten to overcome us. We need to learn to "stick with it." We need to have sufficient faith in ourselves and the patience to persevere with our goals – whether our goal is to pay off our debts, put ourselves through Drama School, or to start and finish that novel that we so dream of writing.

Piscean author James "Celestine Prophecy" Redfield encountered many hitches on his journey to best-seller-dom, and says his motto was "Never, never, never give up." Or as another wise person once said, "Quitters never win. Winners never quit..."

"I am now willing to listen to and act on my dreams."

Dreams

"Dreams are illustrations from the book your soul is writing about you."

Marsha Norman

As Pisceans, our natural astrological realm is the 12th house of the zodiac, that secret, hidden arena where we can duck and dive in the currents of the unconscious and learn to read the secrets of our dreams. Our dreams are often far more vivid and packed with symbols than those of other members of the zodiac, and if we learn to read the symbols right, they can help us live a more authentic and fulfilling life.

When we're grappling with major life decisions, or trying to rid ourselves of self-destructive behaviours, our dreams can also provide valuable clues to the actions we need to take next. A couple of years ago, I dreamed of a court jester holding my hand as I hesitated at the edge of an abyss, encouraging me on, saying: "Jump, I'll help you..." This powerful dream of Mercurial energy (the symbol of the jester) and a "creative leap of faith" gave me the confidence to begin two new writing projects: this book is one of them!

As an exercise, for one week, write down your dreams in your notebook each morning. Read the symbols – use a dream dictionary if you need to. What are your dreams urging you to do today?

"I am now willing to listen to and act on my dreams."

Being In The Flow

"Whether we are happy depends on inner harmony, not on the controls we are able to exert over the great forces of the universe."

Mihaly Csiszentmihaly

As Pisceans, the great secret we need to discover – and the sooner we do this, the better – is that our happiness doesn't depend on anything outside ourselves. So whether we think we need the right person, the right house, the right job, or a credit card with an infinite credit limit – it simply isn't true.

The reality is, we don't need any of these things, because everything we really need already lies deep within us – and we alone hold the key that will unlock our true potential. As those of us who have been fortunate enough to enjoy the experience of "being in the flow" will testify, when you are doing something you totally enjoy, all the distractions and worries of the outside world just fade away…

So your greatest challenge in this lifetime is to discover what it is you can do that will take you to that timeless place where you become totally at one with whatever you are doing. That place where what you are doing is reward enough in itself, regardless of money, regardless of the outcome. This state of being is the ultimate signpost to financial serenity – that state of being where you know that all you have is all you need, and also all that you want. For the simple reason that you now understand that you yourself are enough…

"I do enough, I have enough, I am enough."

Meditations for Women Who Spend Too Much

Index of Meditations

Index

Index

Sources for Quotations

Sources

"SIMPLE ABUNDANCE" © 1995 by Sarah Ban Breathnach. By permission of Warner Books, Inc. Also published by Bantam Press, and used by permission of Transworld Publishers, a division of the Random House Group Limited.

"Money And The Meaning Of Life" © 1991 by Jacob Needleman, reprinted by permission of Doubleday, a division of Bantam Doubleday Dell Publishing Group Inc.

"The Prosperity Secrets of The Ages" © 1964 by Catherine Ponder, published by DeVorss Publishing, Marina del Rey, California.

"The Astrology of Self-Discovery" © 1985 by Tracy Marks. Reprinted by permission of CRCS Publications, Sebastopol, California.

A Gift From The Sea" © 1955 by Anne Morrow Lindbergh, published by Chatto & Windus. Used by permission of Pantheon Books, a division of the Random House Group, Inc. and by permission of The Random House Group Ltd.

"The Power Is Within You"© 1991 by Louise Hay. Used by permission of Hay House Publishing.

"Feng Shui For Your Home" by Sarah Shurety published by Rider. Used by permission of The Random House Group Ltd.

"Money For Life" by Alvin Hall. Reproduced by permission of Hodder & Stoughton Ltd.

"The Palace" by Lisa St. Aubin de Teran. Published by Macmillan Publishers Ltd.

MORE ASTROLOGY CLASSICS FROM LIGHTWORKS PRESS

If you have enjoyed reading this book and would like to learn more about financial astrology, these two classic titles by Jane Bowles are also available by mail order.

MONEY & THE MARKETS
Price £9.99
(by Graham Bates and Jane Bowles)

Since its publication in 1994, this invaluable book has been internationally recognized as THE introduction to financial astrology for the serious student. Contains business case studies, national charts, stock market analysis and a comprehensive guide to the major business and economic cycles.

"This highly readable and instructive book is a valuable starting point, and a worthy successor to David Williams' classic work, Financial Astrology." *(Charles Harvey, Astrological Journal)*

MONEY SIGNS: ASTROLOGY, MONEY AND YOU
Special Offer Price £4.99

The first ever sun sign to astrology and money, with over 25,000 copies sold worldwide. An illuminating journey through the financial strengths and weakness of each sign. Humorous and light hearted, "Money Signs" contains many case studies illustrating the spending, saving and investing styles of each sign.

About The Author

Jane Bowles is an award-winning journalist and author, and the UK's leading writer on financial and business astrology. Jane graduated with Honours in Philosophy, Politics and Economics from St Hilda's College, University of Oxford, and worked as a film and television journalist for Channel Four TV before establishing her career as a free-lance business journalist.

Jane has been drawn to the study of astrology from an early age, and studied with Liz Greene and the late Howard Sasportas at the Centre for Psychological Astrology in London. In the course of her work as a business journalist, she discovered that many investors and traders were using astrology to forecast the world's stock markets and soon became fascinated by the links between astrology and money. Her first book, "Money and the Markets: An Astrological Guide (co-authored with Graham Bates), was published in 1994, and is now recognised as a classic in its field; her second book, "Money Signs: Astrology, Money and You" rapidly became a best-seller in North America.

Jane's work is frequently featured in the UK national press, and she maintains a thriving astrological practice alongside her work as a writer. Jane is currently working on the companion volume to this book "Daily Meditations for Women Who Spend Too Much", and she is also writing a novel about past lives.